DUBAI TRAVEL GUID
Your Ultimate Handbook to Exploring the Captivating City of Luxury and Adventure

By: Melissa J. Norman

TABLE OF CONTENTS

WELCOME TO DUBAI

As the plane touched down at Dubai International Airport, a wave of excitement coursed through me. I couldn't help but grin from ear to ear, knowing that an incredible adventure awaited us in the city of dreams. My two travel buddies, Sarah and Mark, shared my enthusiasm, and we were ready to dive headfirst into the vibrant tapestry that is Dubai.

The moment we stepped out of the airport, the warm desert breeze enveloped us, instantly making us feel at home. We hailed a taxi and embarked on our journey to our hotel, marveling at the futuristic skyline that seemed to stretch endlessly before us. The sight of the iconic Burj Khalifa, piercing the sky like a majestic needle, left us speechless.

Once settled into our accommodations, we wasted no time in exploring the city's wonders. Our first stop was the bustling Dubai Marina, where a vibrant energy permeated the air. We decided to hop on a traditional Abra boat to traverse the sparkling waters, taking in the sight of luxurious yachts and towering skyscrapers that lined the marina. The sun's rays danced on the water, creating a mesmerizing kaleidoscope of colors.

Next on our list was a visit to the historic Al Fahidi neighborhood, where we meandered through narrow lanes adorned with traditional wind towers and beautifully restored heritage buildings. We soaked up the authentic ambiance, exploring quaint art galleries, quaint cafes, and charming boutiques. It was like stepping back in time while still being enveloped by the vibrant spirit of the present.

Our taste buds craved the flavors of the Middle East, and we found ourselves in the vibrant spice and gold souks of Deira. The tantalizing aromas of exotic spices filled the air as we navigated through narrow alleys, marveling at the dazzling displays of gold and precious jewels. We couldn't resist indulging in traditional Emirati cuisine at a local restaurant, savoring mouthwatering dishes like shawarma, hummus, and falafel. Every bite was a burst of flavors that left us craving for more.

But our adventures didn't stop there. The call of the desert was too strong to resist. We embarked on a thrilling desert safari, where we found ourselves soaring over golden dunes in a 4x4 vehicle. The adrenaline rush was palpable as we experienced the exhilarating sport of dune bashing. The vastness of the desert stretched before us, and we couldn't resist the opportunity to try sandboarding, sliding down the dunes like daredevils.

As the sun began to set, we arrived at a Bedouin-style camp in the heart of the desert. We were welcomed with open arms and treated to a mesmerizing evening of entertainment. We watched mesmerizing belly dance performances, marveled at the hypnotic twirls of the tanoura dancers, and savored a sumptuous feast under the starlit sky. The atmosphere was electric, and we found ourselves dancing and laughing with newfound friends.

Dubai had truly cast its spell on us, and we were captivated by its limitless possibilities. From indulging in retail therapy at the world-class shopping malls to taking a stroll along the stunning Palm Jumeirah, every moment was filled with wonder and awe. The blend of luxury, culture, and adventure was the perfect recipe for an unforgettable journey.

As we bid farewell to Dubai, a sense of gratitude washed over us. The memories we made together would forever hold a special place in our hearts. Dubai had welcomed us with open arms, inviting us to immerse ourselves in its captivating spirit. We were travelers, explorers, and now, Dubai enthusiasts. The city had given us a super fun experience, one that would forever be etched in our travel diaries.

Introduction to Dubai

Dubai stands as a testament to human ingenuity and ambition. This dynamic city, with its futuristic skyline and awe-inspiring architectural wonders, has become synonymous with luxury, opulence, and boundless possibilities. As a global hub of commerce, tourism, and innovation, Dubai has carved a prominent place on the world stage, captivating the imaginations of travelers from all corners of the globe.

Dubai's rise from a humble fishing village to a global metropolis is nothing short of remarkable. Situated on the southeastern coast of the Arabian Gulf, this vibrant city is the largest and most populous emirate of the United Arab Emirates

(UAE). Dubai's strategic location between Europe, Asia, and Africa has facilitated its emergence as a vital center for trade and tourism, attracting millions of visitors each year.

One of Dubai's most striking features is its skyline, adorned with architectural masterpieces that defy convention. The crown jewel of this skyline is the iconic Burj Khalifa, the world's tallest building, piercing the heavens at a staggering height. Its gleaming facade and panoramic views from the observation deck offer a glimpse into the city's commitment to pushing boundaries and reaching new heights.

Beyond the skyscrapers, Dubai boasts a diverse tapestry of cultures and experiences. The city's population is a melting pot of nationalities, with residents hailing from around the world. This multicultural environment has given rise to a vibrant cultural scene, where traditional Emirati customs blend harmoniously with influences from various corners of the globe.

Dubai's commitment to preserving its heritage is evident in its historic neighborhoods, such as Al

Fahidi and Bastakiya. These areas offer a glimpse into the city's humble beginnings, with winding alleyways, traditional wind towers, and beautifully restored buildings showcasing the architectural splendor of yesteryears. Strolling through these neighborhoods, visitors can immerse themselves in the rich tapestry of Emirati culture and gain insight into Dubai's history.

As a city that constantly seeks to push boundaries and create unique experiences, Dubai offers an array of world-class attractions and activities. From the man-made wonder of Palm Jumeirah, an island shaped like a palm tree, to the sprawling Dubai Mall, home to an indoor aquarium and an ice rink, there is no shortage of excitement and adventure.

Dubai's desert landscape is an invitation to embark on thrilling adventures. Visitors can indulge in dune bashing, quad biking, and camel riding, or simply bask in the tranquility of the vast golden sands. The city's commitment to excellence is also evident in its golf courses, luxury resorts, and Michelin-starred restaurants, providing a haven for those seeking the epitome of refinement and indulgence.

Dubai's allure is not limited to its tangible attractions; it extends to its warm hospitality and welcoming spirit. The Emirati people are known for their generosity and kindness, ensuring that visitors feel at home in this cosmopolitan oasis.

Geography and Climate

Dubai, located on the southeastern coast of the Arabian Peninsula, is characterized by a unique geography and a desert climate that shapes its landscape and weather patterns. Situated within the Arabian Desert, the city is bordered by the Persian Gulf to the north, while vast stretches of golden sand dunes dominate the southern and eastern parts of the emirate.

The geography of Dubai is marked by contrasting elements. Along the coastline, pristine beaches and azure waters provide a picturesque setting, attracting visitors and residents alike. The city's iconic man-made islands, such as Palm Jumeirah and The World, add a touch of grandeur to the coastline, further enhancing its appeal.

Moving inland, the landscape transitions into the arid and rugged terrain of the desert. Vast expanses of sand dunes, known as "sabkhas," create a dramatic backdrop and offer opportunities for desert adventures and recreational activities.

Dubai experiences a desert climate, characterized by high temperatures, low humidity, and minimal rainfall. The emirate enjoys a sunny weather pattern throughout the year, with long hours of sunshine and blue skies. Summers in Dubai are scorching, with temperatures frequently exceeding 40 degrees Celsius (104 degrees Fahrenheit) during the day. The hot, dry winds from the desert, known as "shamal," can occasionally bring a slight relief from the heat.

Winters in Dubai are mild and pleasant, with average daytime temperatures ranging from 20 to 25 degrees Celsius (68 to 77 degrees Fahrenheit). This season is the peak time for outdoor activities and tourism, as the weather is more comfortable for exploring the city and engaging in various recreational pursuits.

Rainfall in Dubai is scarce, with most precipitation occurring during the winter months. The average annual rainfall is relatively low, typically ranging from 100 to 150 millimeters (3.9 to 5.9 inches), and it is often sporadic and localized.

The History of Dubai

The history of Dubai is a captivating tale of transformation and progress. Originally a small fishing and trading settlement, Dubai's roots can be traced back to the early 19th century. Situated on the southeastern coast of the Arabian Peninsula, the city's strategic location between Europe, Asia, and Africa made it a hub for maritime trade.

In the late 19th century, Dubai became a prominent center for pearling, an industry that played a crucial role in the region's economy. The city's skilled divers ventured into the waters of the Arabian Gulf, risking their lives to harvest pearls that were highly sought after worldwide. The pearling industry brought prosperity to Dubai and shaped its early economic landscape.

The 20th century brought significant changes to Dubai. In the 1930s, the discovery of oil in the region opened up new avenues for growth and development. However, it was the visionary leadership of Sheikh Rashid bin Saeed Al Maktoum, the ruler of Dubai from 1958 to 1990, that truly propelled the city forward.

Under Sheikh Rashid's guidance, Dubai transformed into a global trading and business hub. The ruler's focus on diversifying the economy and investing in infrastructure laid the foundation for Dubai's future success. The development of the Jebel Ali Port and the establishment of free trade zones attracted international businesses, fostering a thriving trade and commerce ecosystem.

In the late 20th century and early 21st century, Dubai's ambition and forward-thinking mindset propelled the city to new heights. The construction of iconic landmarks like the Burj Al Arab, the Palm Jumeirah, and the Burj Khalifa showcased Dubai's commitment to architectural innovation and luxurious living.

Dubai's growth and prosperity have not been limited to physical infrastructure. The city has also emerged as a cultural and tourism destination, hosting international events, such as the Dubai Shopping Festival, Dubai World Cup, and Dubai Expo

2020/2021, which showcased its vibrant arts, entertainment, and hospitality sectors.

Today, Dubai stands as a testament to the resilience, ambition, and vision of its leaders and residents. The city's cosmopolitan character, multicultural society, and relentless pursuit of excellence have made it a global icon and a symbol of progress and possibility.

The Culture of Dubai

The culture of Dubai is a rich tapestry that weaves together elements of traditional Emirati heritage with influences from around the world. Dubai's multicultural society, formed by a diverse expatriate population, has contributed to a vibrant and cosmopolitan cultural landscape.

At the heart of Emirati culture in Dubai lies a deep respect for traditions and customs. Emiratis take great pride in their heritage, reflected in their attire, hospitality, and social values. Traditional dress, such as the flowing white robe called the "kandura" for men and the elegant black "abaya" for women, is still widely worn, particularly on special occasions and national celebrations.

The Arab-Islamic influence is prevalent in Dubai's cultural practices and social norms. Islam is the predominant religion, and mosques are scattered throughout the city, serving as centers of worship and community gathering. The call to prayer resonates across the streets, and the holy month of Ramadan holds special significance, with fasting and charitable acts observed by Muslims.

Dubai's cultural landscape is also shaped by the presence of various ethnic communities and expatriates from around the world. This diversity is celebrated and manifests in the city's culinary scene, where international flavors merge with traditional Emirati dishes. Food festivals and international cuisine offerings showcase the melting pot of flavors that define Dubai's gastronomy.

The arts and entertainment scene in Dubai has experienced significant growth in recent years. The city hosts various cultural events, art exhibitions, and theater performances that bring together local and international talent. The Dubai Opera, a world-class venue, has become a hub for musical performances, theater productions, and ballet.

Hospitality is a fundamental aspect of Dubai's culture, and visitors can experience the warm Emirati welcome firsthand. Traditional Arabian hospitality, known as "gahwa," involves serving Arabic coffee and dates as a gesture of hospitality and goodwill.

Why Visit Dubai in 2023?

If you're contemplating your next adventure, here are compelling reasons why you should visit Dubai in 2023.

First and foremost, Dubai's commitment to innovation and ambition ensures that there's always something new and exciting to experience. The city's skyline is constantly evolving, with groundbreaking architectural wonders continually pushing the boundaries of design. From the iconic Burj Khalifa, the world's tallest building, to the architectural marvels on Palm Jumeirah, Dubai offers a feast for the eyes and a sense of awe-inspiring grandeur.

Dubai is renowned for its world-class shopping experiences, and 2023 promises to take retail therapy to new heights. The city boasts a plethora of luxury malls, boutique shops, and traditional markets, where you can indulge in high-end fashion, exquisite jewelry, and the latest trends. Dubai Shopping Festival, an annual extravaganza, will offer even more enticing discounts, promotions, and entertainment, making it the perfect time to splurge on your favorite brands.

Beyond its luxurious façade, Dubai is a cultural melting pot that celebrates diversity and showcases the best of the Arab world. Immerse yourself in the city's rich heritage by visiting historic neighborhoods like Al Fahidi and Bastakiya, where traditional architecture and museums offer a glimpse into Dubai's past. Explore vibrant souks, where the scents of spices and the buzz of trading activities transport you back in time.

Dubai's commitment to hospitality and world-class entertainment ensures a memorable visit. Indulge in exquisite dining experiences at Michelin-starred restaurants, savoring culinary delights from around the world. Be captivated by dazzling performances at the Dubai Opera or enjoy thrilling adventures in the desert, such as dune bashing and camel riding.

Dubai's pristine beaches, crystal-clear waters, and year-round sunshine make it an ideal destination for relaxation and rejuvenation. Unwind at luxurious beach resorts, soak up the sun, or embark on water-based activities such as yacht cruises, jet skiing, and paddleboarding.

In 2023, Dubai will also be hosting the highly anticipated Expo, a global showcase of innovation, creativity, and cultural exchange. This six-month event will bring together countries from around the world, offering a platform for cutting-edge technologies, immersive exhibitions, and thought-provoking discussions.

Dubai's commitment to safety and infrastructure ensures a seamless and hassle-free visit. The city boasts state-of-the-art transportation systems, world-class healthcare facilities, and a reputation for impeccable service.

About this Guide

Dive into the enchanting world of Dubai with the comprehensive "DUBAI TRAVEL GUIDE 2023." This indispensable companion is designed to elevate your Dubai experience, providing insider tips, local secrets, and invaluable recommendations that will help you immerse yourself in the city's luxury, culture, and adventure.

Discover the breathtaking wonders of Dubai through the pages of this guide. From the iconic landmarks like the Burj Khalifa and Palm Jumeirah to the hidden gems tucked away in historic neighborhoods, this guide unlocks the city's treasures and ensures you make the most of your visit.

Unearth the local secrets that only insiders know. Delve into the vibrant culinary scene and indulge in mouthwatering delicacies at hidden gems favored by locals. Navigate the bustling souks and markets with confidence, knowing the best spots to find unique treasures and bargains.

This guide goes beyond the surface to provide a deeper understanding of Dubai's culture and heritage. Learn about the city's rich history, explore traditional neighborhoods, and witness the fusion of old and new in this cosmopolitan oasis.

Whether you seek adventure in the desert, relaxation on pristine beaches, or a taste of luxury at world-class resorts, this guide offers curated recommendations that cater to your desires. Maximize your time and make informed decisions with practical tips on transportation, accommodations, and safety.

The "DUBAI TRAVEL GUIDE 2023" is your ultimate companion for an unforgettable journey in the jewel of the Middle East. Let it be your trusted advisor, unlocking the city's secrets and guiding you through a truly immersive and captivating Dubai experience.

CHAPTER 1: PLANNING YOUR TRIP TO DUBAI

Planning Your Trip to Dubai can be an exciting and rewarding experience. As you prepare to embark on your journey to this enchanting city, taking the time to plan and organize your trip will ensure a smooth and memorable visit.

Dubai, the cosmopolitan hub of the Middle East, offers a plethora of attractions, experiences, and adventures for every traveler. Whether you're drawn to its stunning architecture, luxurious shopping, vibrant cultural scene, or sun-soaked beaches, careful planning will help you make the most of your time in this captivating destination.

The first step in planning your trip to Dubai is to determine the best time to visit. Consider the weather and temperature preferences, as well as the events and festivals happening during different seasons. Dubai experiences hot summers and mild winters, but each season offers its own unique charm.

Next, decide on the duration of your stay. Dubai's diverse offerings can be experienced within a few days, but if you wish to explore the city in depth or incorporate day trips to nearby attractions, a longer stay might be ideal.

Researching and selecting accommodations that align with your preferences and budget is crucial. Dubai boasts a wide range of options, from luxurious resorts and high-end hotels to budget-friendly accommodations and serviced apartments. Consider the location, amenities, and proximity to attractions when making your choice.

As you plan your itinerary, identify the must-see attractions that pique your interest. From the world-famous Burj Khalifa and Dubai Mall to the historic Al Fahidi Neighborhood and Dubai Creek, there is no shortage of iconic sights to explore. Take into account the time needed to visit each attraction and factor in transportation between locations.

Immersing yourself in Dubai's diverse culinary scene is a must. Research and make reservations at recommended restaurants and cafes to savor both local Emirati dishes and international cuisines.

Lastly, consider any necessary travel documents, such as visas or travel insurance, and familiarize yourself with local customs and etiquette to ensure a respectful and enjoyable experience.

By carefully planning your trip to Dubai, you can create an itinerary that allows you to fully immerse yourself in the city's luxury, culture, and adventure. Prepare for a journey of a lifetime as you explore the wonders and delights of this extraordinary Middle Eastern gem.

When to Go to Dubai

When to go to Dubai depends on your preferences and what you want to experience during your visit. Dubai's climate is characterized by hot summers and mild winters, so choosing the right time of year can make a significant difference in your comfort and the activities available to you.

The winter months, from November to March, are generally considered the best time to visit Dubai. During this period, the temperatures are more moderate, ranging from pleasantly warm to mildly cool. It is the ideal time for outdoor activities, exploring the city's attractions, and enjoying the beautiful beaches. It is also the peak tourist season, so expect larger crowds and higher prices.

If you can tolerate higher temperatures, visiting Dubai during the shoulder seasons of spring (April to May) and autumn (September to October) can offer more affordable prices and fewer tourists. However, temperatures can still be quite hot, so be prepared for the heat if you choose to visit during these times.

The summer months, from June to August, are the hottest and also the off-peak tourist season in Dubai. Temperatures can soar to extreme levels, often exceeding 40 degrees Celsius (104 degrees Fahrenheit). However, if you can handle the heat, you may find discounted rates on accommodations and attractions during this period. It's also a great time to experience indoor attractions and take advantage of air-conditioned malls, theme parks, and entertainment venues.

Another factor to consider is the timing of festivals and events in Dubai. The city hosts various events throughout the year, including the Dubai Shopping

Festival, Dubai Food Festival, and Dubai World Cup, among others. Checking the event calendar can help you plan your visit around specific activities or experiences you're interested in.

Busiest Time To Visit

The busiest time to visit Dubai is during the winter months, from November to March. This period coincides with the peak tourist season when travelers from around the world flock to the city to escape the colder climates of their home countries.

Dubai's pleasant weather during these months, with temperatures ranging from pleasantly warm to mildly cool, makes it an attractive destination for outdoor activities and sightseeing. The comfortable temperatures, combined with the city's myriad attractions and events, draw a large number of visitors.

During the busiest time, Dubai's popular landmarks and attractions can experience larger crowds, longer queues, and higher prices. Iconic sites such as the Burj Khalifa, Dubai Mall, and Palm Jumeirah are particularly bustling with tourists. Additionally, popular tourist activities like desert safaris and dhow cruises may have limited availability or require advance booking.

Hotels and accommodations tend to be in high demand during the peak season, so it's advisable to make reservations well in advance to secure your preferred choices and possibly take advantage of early bird offers.

Despite the increased crowds, visiting Dubai during the busiest time has its advantages. The city is in full swing, and there's a vibrant atmosphere with various events, festivals, and entertainment options to enjoy. The bustling energy and the opportunity to meet people from different cultures create a lively and cosmopolitan ambiance.

If you prefer a more tranquil and relaxed experience, it may be advisable to consider visiting Dubai during the shoulder seasons of spring (April to May) or autumn (September to October), when the city is less crowded, and you can still enjoy favorable weather conditions.

Best Time To Visit in the Summer

Visiting Dubai in the summer can be an adventure for those who can handle the heat and want to take advantage of the off-peak tourist season. While the summer months, from June to August, are the hottest time in Dubai, they can still offer unique experiences and advantages for travelers.

One of the biggest advantages of visiting Dubai in the summer is the opportunity to take advantage of discounted rates on accommodations, flights, and attractions. With fewer tourists during this period, you may find more affordable prices and great deals, allowing you to experience Dubai on a budget.

While temperatures can soar above 40 degrees Celsius (104 degrees Fahrenheit) during the summer, Dubai is well-prepared to combat the heat. The city's infrastructure is equipped with air conditioning, and many outdoor attractions and shopping areas are covered or have shaded areas, providing respite from the sun. Plus, with fewer crowds, you may have more space and comfort to explore indoor attractions like museums, art galleries, and entertainment venues.

Additionally, summer in Dubai is the perfect time to enjoy the city's indoor attractions, such as the world-class malls, theme parks, and indoor ski resorts. You can revel in the thrill of water parks like Aquaventure or explore the wonders of the Dubai Aquarium and Underwater Zoo.

It's important to stay hydrated, wear sunscreen, and plan activities during the cooler parts of the day to beat the heat. Take advantage of early mornings or evenings to explore outdoor attractions or engage in activities like desert safaris or dhow cruises.

Best Time To Visit in Spring

Spring, from March to May, is considered one of the best times to visit Dubai due to its pleasant weather and a range of exciting activities and events. If you're planning a trip to Dubai during the spring season, you can expect comfortable temperatures, clear skies, and a bustling city ready to showcase its charm.

Dubai's spring weather offers a welcome respite from the scorching heat of summer and the milder winter temperatures. During this time, temperatures range from warm to hot, allowing you to explore the city's outdoor attractions, beaches, and desert adventures without feeling overwhelmed by the heat.

One of the highlights of visiting Dubai in the spring is the opportunity to witness the city's vibrant cultural scene. The Dubai Food Festival, held in March, celebrates the culinary diversity of the city, showcasing delicious dishes from around the world. It's a perfect chance to indulge in gastronomic delights and experience the local food culture.

Spring is also a great time for outdoor activities like dhow cruises along Dubai Creek, exploring the historic Al Fahidi Neighborhood, or embarking on desert safaris to experience thrilling adventures amidst the sand dunes.

The pleasant weather during spring makes it ideal for exploring Dubai's iconic landmarks, such as the Burj Khalifa, Dubai Mall, and Palm Jumeirah. You can enjoy sightseeing, take leisurely strolls along the city's promenades, and capture stunning photographs against the backdrop of clear blue skies.

As spring falls outside of the peak tourist season, you can expect fewer crowds and potentially find more affordable accommodations and flight deals. It's a great time to enjoy Dubai's attractions with a bit more space and freedom.

Where to Stay in Dubai

Choosing the right place to stay in Dubai is essential to enhance your overall experience in this vibrant city. With a wide range of accommodations available, each offering its own unique features and advantages, you can find the perfect stay that suits your preferences and budget.

Downtown Dubai is a popular choice for many travelers due to its central location and proximity to iconic landmarks like the Burj Khalifa and Dubai Mall. Here, you'll find luxury hotels and upscale serviced apartments that provide easy access to world-class shopping, dining, and entertainment options.

For a beachside getaway, consider staying in Dubai Marina or Jumeirah Beach Residence (JBR). These areas offer stunning views of the Persian Gulf, luxurious resorts, and a vibrant atmosphere. You can enjoy leisurely walks along the beach promenade, indulge in waterfront dining, and access a range of water sports and activities.

If you're seeking a more traditional and cultural experience, Al Fahidi Historic District and Deira are excellent choices. These neighborhoods showcase the authentic charm of old Dubai, with narrow streets, wind towers, and bustling souks. You can immerse yourself in the local culture, explore traditional markets, and discover the city's rich heritage.

Palm Jumeirah, a man-made island shaped like a palm tree, is another popular area for luxury accommodations. With its stunning beachfront resorts and exclusive amenities, Palm Jumeirah offers a luxurious and indulgent stay.

For a more budget-friendly option, areas like Bur Dubai and Al Barsha provide a range of affordable hotels and apartments while still offering convenient access to major attractions and public transportation.

When choosing where to stay in Dubai, consider factors such as proximity to attractions, preferred atmosphere (urban, beachfront, or traditional), budget, and amenities. It's advisable to book in advance, especially during peak seasons, to secure your preferred choice and take advantage of early booking offers.

What to Do and See in Dubai

During our visit to Dubai, my two friends and I were astounded by the endless array of things to do and see in this remarkable city. From iconic landmarks to thrilling adventures, Dubai truly offers something for everyone.

We started our exploration by visiting the Burj Khalifa, the tallest building in the world. The panoramic views from the observation deck on the 148th floor were absolutely breathtaking. We marveled at the cityscape below and watched as the sun set, painting the sky in vibrant hues.

Another must-visit attraction was the Dubai Mall, a shopper's paradise. We wandered through its vast corridors, indulging in retail therapy and discovering world-renowned brands. The mall's mesmerizing Aquarium and Underwater Zoo left us in awe as we walked through a transparent tunnel surrounded by an array of marine life.

To immerse ourselves in the cultural heritage of Dubai, we explored the historic Al Fahidi Neighborhood. The narrow lanes and traditional wind towers transported us back in time. We visited the Dubai Museum, housed in the Al Fahidi Fort, which provided fascinating insights into the city's history and heritage.

No trip to Dubai would be complete without experiencing the desert. We embarked on a thrilling desert safari, dune bashing in a 4x4 vehicle and sandboarding down the golden slopes. As the sun set, we arrived at a Bedouin-style camp where we enjoyed a delicious Arabian feast, traditional dance performances, and even got henna tattoos.

Dubai's beaches also captivated us. We spent a leisurely day at Jumeirah Beach, soaking up the sun, swimming in the crystal-clear waters, and enjoying beachside refreshments. The Palm Jumeirah, with its luxurious resorts and the incredible Atlantis, The Palm, provided a perfect blend of relaxation and luxury.

To experience the modern side of Dubai, we visited the Dubai Marina, a bustling waterfront area with stunning skyscrapers and a vibrant atmosphere. We took a relaxing boat ride along the marina, admiring the stunning yachts and enjoying the stunning views.

Dubai's culinary scene was a treat for our taste buds. From lavish international buffets to traditional Emirati cuisine, we indulged in a variety of flavors and culinary experiences. The spice markets and food stalls in Deira allowed us to savor local delicacies and immerse ourselves in the aromatic spices of the Middle East.

What to Bring to Dubai

When packing for a trip to Dubai, it's essential to consider the climate and cultural norms of the city. Here are some key items to bring to ensure a comfortable and enjoyable experience:

- Light and breathable clothing: Dubai experiences hot temperatures year-round, so pack lightweight and loose-fitting clothes made from breathable fabrics like cotton or linen. Opt for modest clothing that covers your shoulders and knees, especially when visiting religious sites.

- Sun protection essentials: Don't forget to pack sunscreen with a high SPF, sunglasses, and a hat to protect yourself from the intense sun. These items will come in handy during outdoor activities and beach days.

- Comfortable footwear: With plenty of walking and exploring to do, comfortable shoes are a must. Bring sturdy sandals or sneakers that provide support and are suitable for walking on various terrains.

- Modest swimwear: While Dubai has beautiful beaches and resort pools, it's important to respect the local culture. Pack modest swimwear that covers your body appropriately.

- Light layers: Although Dubai is generally hot, indoor areas like malls and restaurants can be heavily air-conditioned. Pack a light sweater or shawl to keep warm in these cooler environments.

- Travel adapter: Dubai uses a three-pin plug type (Type G), so bring a travel adapter to ensure you can charge your electronic devices.

- Travel documents: Don't forget to bring your passport, visa (if required), travel insurance, and any other necessary documents for your trip.

- Cash and cards: While credit cards are widely accepted in Dubai, it's always handy to have some local currency for smaller transactions or in case of emergencies.

- Medications and personal care items: Bring any necessary medications you require, as well as personal care items like toiletries, hand sanitizer, and insect repellent.

- Respectful attire: Dubai is a city with a strong cultural and religious heritage. Pack modest clothing options for visits to mosques or other religious sites to ensure you respect local customs.

By packing these essentials, you'll be well-prepared for the weather, cultural norms, and activities in Dubai, ensuring a comfortable and enjoyable trip.

CHAPTER 2: GETTING AROUND IN DUBAI

Getting around in Dubai is a breeze thanks to its modern and efficient transportation system. Whether you prefer public transportation or private options, the city offers a range of choices to suit your needs and make navigating Dubai a seamless experience.

One of the most popular modes of transportation in Dubai is the Dubai Metro. The metro system is clean, reliable, and connects key areas of the city, including popular attractions, shopping malls, and business districts. With air-conditioned cabins and separate sections for women and children, it offers a comfortable and safe way to travel.

Another convenient option is the Dubai Tram, which operates in the Dubai Marina and Jumeirah Beach Residence areas. It provides easy access to popular destinations along the coast, making it a great choice for beachgoers and those exploring the vibrant waterfront.

Taxis are readily available throughout the city and offer a convenient way to get around. Dubai's taxis are metered, safe, and operated by professional drivers. Ride-hailing services like Uber and Careem are also popular and provide a hassle-free way to travel, with the added convenience of booking and paying through mobile apps.

For those who prefer more flexibility, renting a car is a viable option in Dubai. The city has well-maintained roads and an extensive network of highways, making it easy to navigate. However, keep in mind that driving in Dubai may require an International Driving Permit, and it's important to familiarize yourself with local traffic rules and regulations.

Additionally, Dubai offers a comprehensive bus network that covers the entire city. Buses are an affordable option and provide access to various neighborhoods and attractions. It's advisable to check the schedules and plan your routes in advance to ensure a smooth journey.

Public Transportation

Public transportation in Dubai is a well-developed and efficient system that provides convenient and reliable options for getting around the city. With a combination of metro, tram, buses, and taxis, navigating Dubai is made easy for residents and visitors alike.

The Dubai Metro is a popular choice for traveling within the city. It is a modern and fully automated system that connects major areas of Dubai, including business districts, shopping malls, and tourist attractions. The metro is clean, safe, and air-conditioned, making it a comfortable option for commuters. It also offers separate cabins for women and children, ensuring a safe and inclusive environment.

The Dubai Tram operates in the Dubai Marina and Jumeirah Beach Residence areas, providing seamless connectivity along the stunning coastline. It is an excellent option for beachgoers and those looking to explore the vibrant waterfront. The tram system is integrated with the metro, allowing for easy transfers between the two modes of transportation.

Dubai's bus network is extensive, covering various neighborhoods and destinations across the city. The buses are air-conditioned and equipped with comfortable seating, offering an affordable way to travel. Bus routes are well-planned and regularly serviced, ensuring efficient transportation throughout the day.

Taxis are readily available in Dubai and provide a convenient door-to-door service. The taxis are metered and operated by professional drivers, ensuring a safe and reliable mode of transportation. Ride-hailing services like Uber and Careem are also popular and offer an additional level of convenience for travelers.

Dubai's public transportation system is integrated and well-connected, making it easy to switch between different modes of transport. Navigating the city is made hassle-free with the availability of public transport apps and websites that provide real-time information on schedules and routes.

Car Rental

Car rental in Dubai offers a convenient and flexible way to explore the city and its surrounding areas at your own pace. With a well-developed road infrastructure and easy access to attractions, renting a car provides freedom and convenience for travelers.

Dubai is home to numerous car rental companies, both international and local, offering a wide range of vehicles to suit different budgets and preferences. From compact cars to luxury sedans and SUVs, you can choose a vehicle that best suits your needs and group size.

Renting a car in Dubai allows you to easily navigate the city's extensive road network, including its modern highways and well-maintained roads. It provides the flexibility to visit attractions at your own schedule and venture beyond the city limits to explore the surrounding areas such as Abu Dhabi or the beautiful Hatta Mountains.

When renting a car in Dubai, it's important to ensure you have a valid driver's license, either from your home country or an International Driving Permit. You should also be aware of the local traffic rules and regulations to ensure a safe and smooth driving experience.

Most car rental companies in Dubai offer comprehensive insurance coverage and roadside assistance for added peace of mind. Additionally, they provide options for picking up and dropping off the vehicle at convenient locations, such as airports or city centers.

It's advisable to book your car rental in advance, especially during peak seasons, to secure the vehicle of your choice and take advantage of any early booking offers or discounts.

Buses

Buses in Dubai form an integral part of the city's public transportation system, providing residents and visitors with a convenient and affordable way to travel around the city. Dubai's bus network is extensive, covering a wide range of routes and destinations, making it a reliable option for exploring the city and its various neighborhoods.

Dubai's buses are modern, comfortable, and air-conditioned, offering a pleasant commuting experience. They are equipped with amenities such as comfortable seating, designated spaces for people with disabilities, and CCTV cameras for added safety and security.

The bus routes in Dubai are well-planned and efficiently serviced, ensuring regular and reliable transportation throughout the day. They cover key areas of the city, including business districts, residential areas, shopping malls, and popular tourist attractions. Whether you want to visit the iconic Burj Khalifa, explore the historic Al Fahidi Neighborhood, or indulge in retail therapy at the Dubai Mall, there's likely a bus route that will take you there.

Dubai's bus system is also integrated with other modes of public transportation, such as the metro and tram, allowing for seamless transfers and convenient connections between different parts of the city.

To make traveling by bus even more convenient, Dubai's Roads and Transport Authority (RTA) has developed user-friendly apps and online platforms that provide real-time information on bus schedules, routes, and fares. This enables passengers to plan their journeys in advance and track the arrival and departure times of buses.

Travel Tips

When planning your trip to Dubai, it's helpful to keep a few travel tips in mind to ensure a smooth and enjoyable experience in this dynamic city:

1. Respect the local culture: Dubai is an Islamic city with strong cultural and religious values. It's important to dress modestly, especially when visiting religious sites and public places. Be mindful of local customs and traditions, and always show respect for the local culture.

2. Check visa requirements: Before traveling to Dubai, make sure to check the visa requirements for your country of residence. Depending on your nationality, you may need to obtain a visa in advance or upon arrival. Ensure that your passport has a sufficient validity period to meet the entry requirements.

3. Stay hydrated: Dubai's climate can be hot and dry, especially during the summer months.

Stay hydrated by drinking plenty of water throughout the day. Carry a water bottle with you and take advantage of the numerous drinking water stations available across the city.

4. Be mindful of the weather: Dubai experiences scorching summers, so it's important to plan outdoor activities during the cooler parts of the day. Keep track of the weather forecast and dress appropriately to protect yourself from the sun.

5. Follow local laws and regulations: Familiarize yourself with the local laws and regulations in Dubai. Respect traffic rules, refrain from public displays of affection, and avoid consuming alcohol in public areas outside designated venues. It's important to abide by the laws to ensure a trouble-free stay.

6. Use reliable transportation: Dubai has a well-developed public transportation system, including the metro, buses, trams, and taxis. Utilize these reliable modes of transportation

to navigate the city conveniently and efficiently. Use licensed taxis or ride-hailing services for private transportation needs.

7. Stay connected: Dubai has excellent connectivity with Wi-Fi available in most hotels, restaurants, and public places. Consider purchasing a local SIM card for your phone to have access to data and stay connected during your trip.

Shopping and Nightlife

Dubai is renowned as a shopper's paradise, offering a wide array of shopping experiences to suit every taste and budget. From traditional souks to modern malls, the city has it all.

Dubai's malls are a shopaholic's dream come true. The city is home to some of the world's largest and most luxurious shopping centers, such as The Dubai Mall, Mall of the Emirates, and Ibn Battuta Mall. These malls house an impressive selection of international and local brands, ranging from high-end fashion to electronics and everything in between. With their air-conditioned interiors, entertainment options, and dining establishments, these malls provide a complete shopping experience.

For a more traditional shopping experience, explore Dubai's vibrant souks. The Gold Souk, Perfume Souk, and Spice Souk are must-visit destinations for those looking to immerse themselves in the city's rich culture and heritage. Here, you can find intricate gold jewelry, exotic spices, and fragrant perfumes, making for unique and memorable souvenirs.

Dubai's nightlife scene is equally enticing, offering an array of entertainment options for night owls. From glamorous rooftop bars with breathtaking views to buzzing nightclubs that host world-class DJs, there is no shortage of options to dance the night away. Many hotels also offer sophisticated lounges and live music venues, creating a vibrant and diverse nightlife scene that caters to different tastes.

It's important to note that Dubai's nightlife adheres to certain regulations and guidelines. Alcohol consumption is primarily limited to licensed venues, such as hotels and restaurants, and public displays of affection should be avoided.

Whether you're a shopaholic or a nightlife enthusiast, Dubai has something for everyone. Explore the city's glamorous malls, haggle for treasures in the traditional souks, and indulge in the exciting nightlife offerings. Dubai's shopping and nightlife scene are sure to leave you with unforgettable memories and experiences.

Food and Drink

Dubai is a culinary melting pot that offers a diverse range of culinary experiences, catering to every palate and preference. From traditional Emirati cuisine to international delicacies, the city is a haven for food lovers.

Dubai boasts a thriving food scene with restaurants run by renowned chefs from around the world. You can savor exquisite fine dining experiences in upscale establishments that showcase innovative and fusion cuisines. These restaurants offer a blend of flavors and techniques, ensuring a memorable gastronomic journey.

For those seeking a taste of authentic Emirati cuisine, Dubai's local eateries and cafes are a must-visit. Sample dishes like Machboos (spiced rice with meat or seafood), Harees (a wheat and meat porridge), and Luqaimat (sweet dumplings). These traditional flavors provide a unique glimpse into the local culture and culinary heritage.

Dubai is also famous for its bustling food markets, such as the Spice Souk and the Fish Market. Explore these vibrant markets to discover a wide variety of spices, fresh seafood, fruits, and vegetables. You can even try your hand at haggling for the best prices while immersing yourself in the vibrant atmosphere.

When it comes to beverages, Dubai offers a range of options to quench your thirst. Traditional Arabic coffee (gahwa) and tea (chai) are commonly served in local establishments and provide a taste of the region's hospitality. Fresh fruit juices and smoothies are also popular, with numerous juice bars and cafes offering refreshing concoctions.

Dubai's food and beverage scene caters to all budgets, from street food stalls to luxurious dining experiences. No matter your culinary preferences,

Dubai offers a world of flavors and culinary delights waiting to be discovered.

Traditional Dishes

Dubai's culinary scene is a beautiful reflection of its rich cultural heritage, and exploring traditional dishes is an essential part of immersing yourself in the local culture. Here are some traditional dishes in Dubai that you should try:

Machboos: This flavorful dish is a staple in Emirati cuisine. It consists of fragrant rice cooked with tender meat (usually chicken, lamb, or fish) and a blend of aromatic spices such as saffron, cardamom, and cinnamon. The dish is often garnished with fried onions and served with a side of tangy yogurt.

Harees: Harees is a hearty dish made from a combination of ground wheat and meat (typically chicken or lamb). The ingredients are slow-cooked together until they form a thick and creamy porridge-like consistency. Harees is traditionally enjoyed during special occasions and celebrations.

Luqaimat: These sweet dumplings are a popular Emirati dessert. Made from a dough of flour, sugar, and yeast, the dumplings are deep-fried until golden brown and then drizzled with date syrup and sprinkled with sesame seeds. Luqaimat are small, light, and delightfully sweet, making them a favorite indulgence among locals and visitors alike.

Majboos: Similar to the popular Indian dish biryani, Majboos is a flavorful rice dish cooked with a combination of spices, meat (chicken, lamb, or fish), and vegetables. The aromatic blend of spices and the tender meat make Majboos a true culinary delight.

Balaleet: Balaleet is a unique Emirati breakfast dish that combines sweet and savory flavors. It consists of vermicelli noodles cooked with saffron, cardamom, and rose water, and then topped with a layer of lightly sweetened omelet. Balaleet is often served with a side of date syrup or fresh fruits.

Trying these traditional dishes in Dubai allows you to experience the authentic flavors and culinary heritage of the region. Whether you're a food enthusiast or a curious traveler, exploring the local cuisine is a delightful journey that unveils the cultural richness of Dubai's gastronomy.

Eating Out

Eating out in Dubai is a culinary adventure that caters to all tastes and preferences. The city boasts a vibrant dining scene with an array of restaurants, cafes, and eateries offering cuisines from around the world. Here's a glimpse into the experience of eating out in Dubai:

Dubai is known for its diverse culinary offerings, ranging from local Emirati delicacies to international flavors. You'll find everything from upscale fine dining establishments helmed by world-renowned chefs to casual street food stalls serving up delicious bites. Whether you're in the mood for authentic Emirati cuisine, Middle Eastern specialties, Asian fusion, European classics, or any other global cuisine, Dubai has it all.

The city is home to a wide range of restaurants, each with its own unique ambiance and style. You can dine in elegant establishments with stunning views of the city skyline, enjoy al fresco meals on waterfront promenades, or immerse yourself in the vibrant atmosphere of bustling food markets and food trucks.

Dubai also offers a variety of dining experiences to suit different budgets. From lavish dining experiences in renowned Michelin-starred restaurants to affordable local eateries and street food stalls, there's something for every wallet.

Another highlight of eating out in Dubai is the emphasis on quality and service. The city prides itself on offering exceptional culinary experiences, with many restaurants striving to provide top-notch service and memorable dining moments. The staff is often knowledgeable, friendly, and attentive, ensuring that your dining experience is nothing short of exceptional.

Dubai's dining scene is also known for its innovation, with many restaurants pushing the boundaries of gastronomy. You can find unique dining concepts such as underwater restaurants, rooftop bars, and themed eateries that offer an immersive experience alongside delectable dishes.

CHAPTER 3: WHAT TO DO BEFORE TRAVELING

Before embarking on your journey to Dubai, it's important to take certain steps and make necessary preparations to ensure a smooth and enjoyable travel experience. Here are some essential things to do before traveling to Dubai:

Check passport and visa requirements: Ensure that your passport is valid for at least six months beyond your planned departure date. Check the visa requirements for your country of residence and apply for a visa if necessary. Dubai offers visa-on-arrival for citizens of certain countries, but it's always best to verify the requirements beforehand.

Research and plan your itinerary: Dubai offers a plethora of attractions and activities, so it's a good idea to research and plan your itinerary in advance. Determine the top sights, landmarks, and experiences you don't want to miss and create a schedule that suits your preferences.

Arrange accommodation: Dubai offers a wide range of accommodation options, from luxury hotels to budget-friendly accommodations. Research and book your accommodation based on your preferences, budget, and location preferences. It's advisable to book in advance, especially during peak travel seasons.

Pack appropriately: Consider the weather and cultural norms when packing for Dubai. Lightweight and breathable clothing is suitable for the hot climate, but it's important to respect local customs and dress modestly in public areas. Don't forget essentials like sunscreen, a hat, and comfortable shoes for exploring the city.

Check health and safety recommendations: Prioritize your health and safety by checking the latest travel advisories and recommendations for Dubai. Make sure you have appropriate travel insurance coverage and consult a healthcare professional for any required vaccinations.

Exchange currency: While credit cards are widely accepted in Dubai, it's a good idea to have some local currency (UAE Dirham) for small purchases and emergencies. Exchange currency before your trip or upon arrival at the airport.

Entry Requirement

When planning your trip to Dubai, it's crucial to understand the entry requirements to ensure a hassle-free journey. Here's a brief overview of the entry requirements for visiting Dubai:

Passport: Ensure that your passport is valid for at least six months beyond your intended stay in Dubai. This is a mandatory requirement for entry into the country.

Visa: Depending on your nationality, you may require a visa to enter Dubai. Citizens of several countries are eligible for visa-on-arrival, which allows for a stay of up to 30 days. However, it's essential to check the visa requirements specific to your country of residence before traveling. Alternatively, you may need to apply for a visa in advance through the UAE embassy or consulate.

COVID-19 Protocols: Due to the ongoing pandemic, additional entry requirements may be in place. It is crucial to stay updated on the latest COVID-19 travel guidelines and protocols set by the UAE government and the Dubai authorities. These may include pre-travel PCR testing, health declaration forms, and mandatory quarantine measures.

Health Insurance: While not a mandatory requirement, it is strongly recommended to have travel health insurance that covers medical expenses and emergencies during your stay in Dubai.

Return Ticket and Proof of Accommodation: It is advisable to have a return ticket and proof of accommodation, such as hotel reservations or an invitation from a host, as it may be requested by immigration officials upon arrival.

Travel Insurance

Travel insurance is a crucial component of any trip, and it holds particular significance when visiting Dubai. With its vibrant attractions, diverse activities, and potential unforeseen circumstances, having travel insurance provides peace of mind and financial protection. Here's a brief overview of travel insurance considerations for Dubai:

Medical Coverage: Ensure that your travel insurance includes comprehensive medical coverage. This should cover medical expenses, hospitalization, emergency medical evacuation, and repatriation. Dubai has excellent healthcare facilities, but medical costs can be high, so having adequate coverage is essential.

COVID-19 Coverage: Given the ongoing pandemic, it is vital to check if your travel insurance provides coverage for COVID-19-related medical expenses. This coverage may include testing, treatment, quarantine costs, and trip cancellation due to COVID-19.

Trip Cancellation or Interruption: Look for travel insurance that offers coverage for trip cancellation or interruption due to unexpected events like illness, injury, family emergencies, or travel restrictions. This coverage can reimburse you for non-refundable expenses such as flights, accommodation, and pre-booked activities.

Baggage and Personal Belongings: Ensure that your travel insurance provides coverage for lost, stolen, or damaged baggage and personal belongings. This coverage can help replace or reimburse you for the value of your items.

Travel Delays and Missed Connections: Travel insurance that covers travel delays and missed connections can be invaluable. It can compensate you for additional expenses incurred due to unexpected flight delays, cancellations, or missed connections, such as accommodation, meals, and alternative transportation.

Familiarize Yourself with the Currency

Familiarizing yourself with the currency in Dubai is essential for a smooth and hassle-free experience during your visit. Here's a brief overview to help you understand the currency in Dubai:

The official currency of Dubai is the UAE Dirham (AED). It is abbreviated as "إ.د" or "AED" and is commonly referred to as the "Dirham." The Dirham is further divided into smaller units called fils, with 100 fils equaling 1 Dirham.

When visiting Dubai, it's important to have a basic understanding of the currency and its denominations. The commonly used banknotes are in denominations of 5, 10, 20, 50, 100, 200, 500, and 1000 Dirhams, while coins are available in denominations of 1 Dirham and smaller values like 50, 25, 10, and 5 fils.

Currency exchange services are widely available in Dubai, including at airports, banks, exchange bureaus, and hotels. It's advisable to exchange your currency at authorized outlets to ensure fair rates and avoid counterfeit notes. You may also withdraw cash from ATMs, which are conveniently located throughout the city.

Credit and debit cards are widely accepted in Dubai, including major international brands such as Visa, Mastercard, and American Express. However, it's a good idea to carry some cash for smaller purchases, street markets, and establishments that may not accept cards.

Before your trip, it's recommended to check the current exchange rates and consider notifying your bank about your travel plans to ensure uninterrupted card usage.

General Safety Tips

While Dubai is generally considered a safe destination for travelers, it's always wise to be aware of your surroundings and take necessary precautions. Here are some general safety tips to keep in mind during your stay:

Respect Local Laws and Customs: Familiarize yourself with the local laws, regulations, and customs in Dubai. Observe cultural norms, dress modestly in public places, and avoid engaging in activities that may be considered offensive or illegal.

Personal Belongings: Keep your personal belongings, including passports, wallets, and electronic devices, secure at all times. Avoid displaying large sums of cash or valuable items in public, and use hotel safes or secure lockers when available.

Public Transportation: When using public transportation, be mindful of your belongings and stay vigilant against pickpocketing. Avoid traveling alone late at night and consider using licensed taxis or ride-hailing services for added safety.

Road Safety: Dubai has well-maintained roads and a strict traffic system. Follow traffic rules, use designated crosswalks, and exercise caution when crossing the streets. If driving, adhere to speed limits, wear seat belts, and avoid using mobile phones while driving.

Extreme Weather: Dubai experiences hot and humid weather, particularly during the summer months. Stay hydrated, wear lightweight and breathable clothing, and use sunscreen to protect yourself from the sun's rays. During sandstorms or heavy rains, follow local advisories and seek shelter if necessary.

Emergency Services: Familiarize yourself with the local emergency contact numbers, including those for police, ambulance, and fire services. Keep important contact numbers and addresses handy, including your embassy or consulate.

COVID-19 Precautions: Stay updated on the latest COVID-19 guidelines and protocols issued by the Dubai authorities. Follow hygiene practices such as wearing masks, practicing social distancing, and frequently sanitizing your hands.

Health Safety Consideration

Health safety is an important aspect to consider when visiting Dubai to ensure a pleasant and worry-free trip. Here are some health safety considerations to keep in mind during your stay:

COVID-19 Guidelines: Stay updated on the latest COVID-19 guidelines and regulations issued by the Dubai authorities. Follow the recommended safety measures, such as wearing masks in public places, practicing social distancing, and frequent hand hygiene. Be aware of any testing or quarantine requirements that may be in place.

Medical Facilities: Dubai has excellent healthcare facilities with well-equipped hospitals and clinics. It is advisable to have travel insurance that covers medical expenses in case of illness or injury. Keep a list of emergency contact numbers, including the nearest hospitals or medical centers, and carry any necessary medications with you.

Hygiene Practices: Maintain good hygiene practices during your trip. Wash your hands frequently with soap and water for at least 20 seconds, or use hand sanitizers when soap is not available. Avoid touching your face, especially your eyes, nose, and mouth, to minimize the risk of infections.

Safe Food and Water: Dubai generally has safe food and water standards. However, it is recommended to drink bottled water and consume food from reputable establishments to reduce the risk of foodborne illnesses. Ensure that fruits and vegetables are properly washed and cooked, and avoid street food that may not meet hygiene standards.

Sun Safety: Dubai experiences a hot climate, so protect yourself from the sun's harmful rays. Wear sunscreen with a high SPF, seek shade during peak sun hours, and stay hydrated by drinking plenty of water.

Travel Health Insurance: Consider obtaining travel health insurance that covers medical emergencies, including hospitalization and medical evacuation. Check the policy details to ensure it covers any pre-existing conditions or specific activities you plan to engage in during your trip.

CHAPTER 4: EXPLORING DUBAI'S LANDMARKS

Dubai is a city renowned for its extraordinary landmarks that capture the essence of its modernity, opulence, and cultural heritage. Exploring these iconic landmarks is an absolute must for any visitor to Dubai. Let's delve into some of the city's most notable landmarks:

Burj Khalifa, the tallest building in the world, is a towering testament to Dubai's architectural prowess. Ascend to its observation decks and marvel at the panoramic views of the city's skyline. Adjacent to the Burj Khalifa, the Dubai Mall offers an unparalleled shopping experience, featuring an extensive array of luxury brands, entertainment attractions, and the captivating Dubai Aquarium and Underwater Zoo.

Venture to the Palm Jumeirah, an artificial island shaped like a palm tree, and revel in its lavish resorts, upscale villas, and pristine beaches. A traditional boat ride along Dubai Creek provides an opportunity to immerse yourself in the city's historical charm, with bustling souks and traditional markets lining its shores.

Visit the Jumeirah Mosque, an architectural gem and one of the few mosques open to non-Muslim visitors. Explore its intricately designed interior and gain insights into Islamic culture through guided tours.

Dubai Marina offers a vibrant waterfront experience, with a stunning marina surrounded by striking skyscrapers. Take leisurely strolls along the promenade, savor delectable cuisine at waterfront restaurants, or embark on a serene boat cruise.

Iconic Skyscrapers: Burj Khalifa and Burj Al Arab

Dubai is home to two iconic skyscrapers that have become synonymous with the city's architectural marvels: the Burj Khalifa and the Burj Al Arab. These towering structures have redefined the skyline and captured the imagination of visitors from around the world.

The Burj Khalifa stands as the tallest building in the world, soaring to an incredible height of 828 meters.

Its sleek design and shimmering facade make it an architectural masterpiece. Visitors can journey to its observation decks on the 124th and 148th floors to witness breathtaking panoramic views of Dubai. The Burj Khalifa is not just a feat of engineering; it's a symbol of Dubai's ambition, innovation, and modernity.

The Burj Al Arab, often referred to as the world's only seven-star hotel, is an iconic symbol of luxury and extravagance. Shaped like the sail of a dhow, a traditional Arabian sailing vessel, this striking building sits on its own man-made island. Its opulent interiors, lavish suites, and impeccable service have earned it a reputation as one of the most luxurious hotels in the world. Even if you're not staying at the Burj Al Arab, you can still admire its magnificent architecture from the outside and capture memorable photos.

Both the Burj Khalifa and the Burj Al Arab showcase Dubai's relentless pursuit of architectural excellence and its desire to push boundaries. They have become iconic landmarks that symbolize the city's modernity, grandeur, and status as a global destination. A visit to Dubai is incomplete without witnessing the awe-inspiring presence of these architectural giants.

Dubai Marina and Palm Jumeirah

Dubai Marina and Palm Jumeirah are two extraordinary man-made developments that have transformed Dubai's coastline and captivated visitors with their grandeur and beauty.

Dubai Marina is a vibrant waterfront district that features a stunning marina dotted with luxurious yachts and surrounded by breathtaking skyscrapers. It offers a unique lifestyle experience with its waterfront promenade, upscale restaurants, trendy cafes, and glamorous shopping destinations. Stroll along the marina, soak in the bustling atmosphere, and enjoy panoramic views of the surrounding architecture. Dubai Marina is also known for its exciting nightlife, with an array of bars and clubs that come alive after the sun sets.

Palm Jumeirah, shaped like a palm tree, is an iconic artificial island that has become a symbol of Dubai's ambition and innovation. This palm-shaped archipelago is home to lavish resorts, prestigious villas, and pristine beaches. Take a monorail ride along the palm fronds to witness the magnificent views and appreciate the sheer scale of this remarkable engineering feat. Relax on the palm-fringed beaches, indulge in water sports, or savor world-class dining at one of the island's renowned restaurants. Palm Jumeirah offers an oasis of luxury and tranquility amidst the vibrant energy of Dubai.

The Dubai Mall and Mall of the Emirates

The Dubai Mall, located in the heart of Downtown Dubai, is one of the world's largest shopping malls. It offers an unparalleled shopping experience with a vast array of luxury brands, fashion boutiques, electronics stores, and department stores. The mall also features various entertainment attractions, including the mesmerizing Dubai Aquarium and Underwater Zoo, the VR Park, and the Dubai Ice Rink. Visitors can explore the mall's sprawling fashion avenue, indulge in gourmet dining options, or enjoy the magnificent Dubai Fountain show just outside its doors.

Mall of the Emirates is another retail paradise that boasts an impressive collection of high-end fashion brands, lifestyle stores, and department stores. What sets it apart is its renowned indoor ski resort, Ski Dubai, where visitors can experience snow activities in the middle of the desert. The mall also offers a wide range of entertainment options, including a multiplex cinema and a multitude of restaurants and cafes.

Both malls go beyond traditional shopping experiences by combining retail therapy with entertainment, dining, and cultural attractions. They showcase Dubai's commitment to creating extravagant and immersive environments for visitors to indulge in. Whether you're seeking the latest fashion trends, world-class entertainment, or simply a delightful shopping experience, The Dubai Mall and Mall of the Emirates are must-visit destinations that cater to every shopper's desires.

Dubai Creek and Old Dubai

Dubai Creek and Old Dubai are historical gems that offer a glimpse into the city's rich heritage and traditional charm. Situated at the heart of the city, Dubai Creek has played a pivotal role in the development of Dubai as a trading hub.

Dubai Creek is a natural seawater inlet that divides the city into two main sections: Deira and Bur Dubai. Take an enchanting abra (traditional wooden boat) ride along the creek and immerse yourself in the sights and sounds of the bustling waterway. Admire the juxtaposition of old and new as you pass by traditional dhows (Arabian sailing vessels) and modern skyscrapers.

On the Bur Dubai side of Dubai Creek lies Old Dubai, a district steeped in history. Explore the historic Al Fahidi neighborhood, known for its traditional wind-tower houses and narrow alleys. Visit the Dubai Museum housed in the 18th-century Al Fahidi Fort, which provides a captivating insight into Dubai's transformation from a fishing village to a global metropolis.

Wander through the vibrant souks (markets) of Deira, such as the Gold Souk and Spice Souk, where you can haggle for exotic spices and admire glittering displays of gold and jewelry. These bustling markets are a sensory feast, offering a glimpse into the vibrant trade and commerce that has thrived in Dubai for centuries.

Cultural Experiences: Dubai Museum and Jumeirah Mosque

The Dubai Museum, located in the historic Al Fahidi Fort, is a captivating journey into the city's past. Step inside this 18th-century fort, and you'll find a treasure trove of artifacts, exhibits, and immersive displays that tell the story of Dubai's transformation from a humble fishing village to a modern metropolis. Explore the traditional courtyard houses, learn about the pearl diving industry, and marvel at the fascinating archaeological discoveries. The museum provides a deep insight into the Emirati culture, traditions, and way of life.

For a deeper understanding of Islamic culture, a visit to the Jumeirah Mosque is a must. This stunning mosque is one of the few in Dubai that welcomes non-Muslim visitors. Join a guided tour to learn about Islamic practices, traditions, and architecture. The mosque's intricate design, adorned with beautiful calligraphy and stunning geometric patterns, is a sight to behold. It's an opportunity to gain a greater appreciation for the religion and the values that shape the local community.

These cultural experiences offer a glimpse into the roots and values that underpin Dubai's society. They provide an enriching opportunity to learn about the city's heritage, customs, and traditions. Immerse yourself in the history and spirituality of Dubai through visits to the Dubai Museum and the Jumeirah Mosque, and gain a deeper appreciation for the cultural tapestry of the city.

CHAPTER 5: BEYOND DUBAI (Day Trips and Nearby Destinations)

While Dubai offers an abundance of attractions and experiences, venturing beyond the city's limits unveils a world of incredible day trips and nearby destinations waiting to be explored.

One popular day trip from Dubai is a visit to Abu Dhabi, the capital of the United Arab Emirates. Just a short drive away, Abu Dhabi offers a captivating blend of tradition and modernity. Marvel at the magnificent Sheikh Zayed Grand Mosque, stroll along the glamorous Corniche, and immerse yourself in the cultural riches of the Louvre Abu Dhabi. The city also boasts thrilling theme parks like Ferrari World and Yas Waterworld, perfect for an adrenaline-filled adventure.

For nature lovers, a trip to the stunning Hajar Mountains is a must. Located on the eastern coast of the United Arab Emirates, this mountain range is a paradise for outdoor enthusiasts. Embark on a hiking or off-roading expedition, soak in the natural hot springs of Fujairah, or simply revel in the breathtaking landscapes and picturesque wadis (dry riverbeds).

Another remarkable day trip is a visit to the enchanting desert dunes surrounding Dubai. Experience the thrill of dune bashing in a 4x4 vehicle, ride a camel through the golden sands, or enjoy a traditional Bedouin-style dinner under the starry desert sky.

Dubai's strategic location also allows for easy access to other countries in the region. Explore the ancient wonders of Oman's capital, Muscat, or take a trip to the bustling metropolis of Doha, Qatar, with its stunning architecture and vibrant cultural scene.

Abu Dhabi: Sheikh Zayed Grand Mosque and Louvre Abu Dhabi

Abu Dhabi, the capital of the United Arab Emirates, is a city brimming with architectural marvels and cultural treasures. Two standout attractions that must be experienced are the Sheikh Zayed Grand Mosque and the Louvre Abu Dhabi.

The Sheikh Zayed Grand Mosque is a breathtaking masterpiece that showcases the grandeur of Islamic architecture. It is one of the largest mosques in the world and an iconic symbol of Abu Dhabi. Step inside this magnificent structure and be awestruck by its opulent design, adorned with intricate carvings, sparkling chandeliers, and the world's largest hand-knotted carpet. The serene ambiance and the play of light and shadow create a mesmerizing atmosphere that invites contemplation and reverence. The mosque welcomes visitors of all backgrounds and offers a truly immersive cultural experience.

The Louvre Abu Dhabi, an architectural wonder in itself, is a cultural beacon that bridges the gap between East and West. This innovative museum showcases a diverse collection of art and artifacts from around the world. Explore the galleries and encounter masterpieces spanning centuries and civilizations. The museum's stunning design, with its mesmerizing dome that filters light to create a "rain of light" effect, adds to the allure of the exhibits. From ancient sculptures to modern paintings, the Louvre Abu Dhabi offers a captivating journey through human creativity and heritage.

A visit to Abu Dhabi to witness the Sheikh Zayed Grand Mosque and explore the Louvre Abu Dhabi is an enriching experience that unveils the city's commitment to art, culture, and architectural splendor. It's a chance to immerse yourself in the magnificence of human achievement and appreciate the cultural treasures that Abu Dhabi has to offer.

Sharjah: Cultural Capital of the UAE

Sharjah, known as the "Cultural Capital of the UAE," is a captivating city that proudly preserves and celebrates its rich heritage and artistic traditions. Located just a short distance from Dubai, Sharjah offers a unique and authentic cultural experience that should not be missed.

One of the highlights of Sharjah is its impressive array of museums and cultural institutions. The Sharjah Art Museum is a hub for contemporary and traditional art, showcasing the works of local and international artists. The Sharjah Museum of Islamic Civilization is a treasure trove of Islamic art, artifacts, and historical exhibits that provide insights into the region's rich heritage. Other notable museums include the Sharjah Heritage Museum, Sharjah Calligraphy Museum, and Sharjah

Archaeology Museum, each offering a unique perspective on the city's cultural legacy.

Sharjah's commitment to promoting literature and education is evident in its status as the UNESCO World Book Capital for 2019. The city hosts the annual Sharjah International Book Fair, attracting bibliophiles from around the world. The charming Sharjah Heritage Area, with its restored traditional houses, narrow alleys, and vibrant souks, transports visitors back in time to experience the authentic Emirati culture.

The city also hosts a plethora of cultural festivals and events throughout the year. The Sharjah Light Festival illuminates the city's landmarks with stunning light displays, while the Sharjah Biennial showcases contemporary art from around the world. The Sharjah Islamic Arts Festival, Sharjah Heritage Days, and the Sharjah International Film Festival further contribute to the city's vibrant cultural scene.

Sharjah's commitment to preserving its cultural heritage is evident in its strict preservation laws, which have helped maintain its traditional architecture and authentic charm. The city's efforts have earned it the title of the "Cultural Capital of the Arab World" by UNESCO in 1998.

For those seeking an immersive cultural experience, a visit to Sharjah is a must. Immerse yourself in the city's rich artistic heritage, explore its fascinating museums, and witness its vibrant cultural events. Sharjah offers a unique glimpse into the traditions and values that have shaped the United Arab Emirates, making it a true cultural gem of the region.

Al Ain: Oasis City and UNESCO World Heritage Sites

Al Ain, often referred to as the "Oasis City," is a hidden gem nestled in the desert of the United Arab Emirates. This charming city is renowned for its lush greenery, ancient forts, and fascinating UNESCO World Heritage Sites, offering visitors a unique glimpse into the region's rich history and natural beauty.

At the heart of Al Ain lies the Al Ain Oasis, a serene and verdant paradise that showcases the ingenuity of traditional falaj irrigation systems. Stroll through the palm tree-lined pathways and discover ancient agricultural practices that have sustained this oasis for centuries. The oasis is not only a tranquil retreat but also a living testament to the deep connection between people and nature in the Arabian Peninsula.

Al Ain is also home to several UNESCO World Heritage Sites, including the historic Al Ain Fort (also known as Al Jahili Fort). This magnificent fortress, built in the late 19th century, served as a defense stronghold and has now been transformed into a captivating museum that delves into the region's history and culture. The fort's impressive architecture and picturesque surroundings make it a must-visit for history enthusiasts and architecture admirers alike.

Another UNESCO World Heritage Site in Al Ain is the Hili Archaeological Park, an ancient settlement dating back over 4,000 years. Explore the well-preserved tombs, ancient houses, and archaeological remnants that offer insights into the city's prehistoric past.

Beyond its historical and cultural attractions, Al Ain also boasts stunning natural landscapes. The Jebel Hafeet mountain, rising over 1,200 meters, provides breathtaking panoramic views of the city and surrounding desert. The Al Ain Zoo, with its extensive collection of wildlife, is a popular destination for animal lovers.

Al Ain's unique blend of natural beauty and cultural heritage makes it a captivating destination for travelers seeking an authentic and immersive experience. Whether you're exploring the lush oasis, marveling at ancient forts, or taking in the majestic mountain vistas, Al Ain promises an unforgettable journey through the rich tapestry of the United Arab Emirates' history and natural wonders.

CHAPTER 6: UNVEILING DUBAI'S CULTURE AND TRADITIONS

Unveiling Dubai's Culture and Traditions takes you on a fascinating journey into the heart and soul of this vibrant city, going beyond its gleaming skyscrapers and luxurious lifestyle. Delve into the rich cultural tapestry and centuries-old traditions that define the essence of Dubai.

Dubai may be renowned as a global metropolis, but it has managed to preserve its cultural heritage amidst rapid modernization. This guide invites you to explore the multifaceted aspects of Dubai's culture, from its traditional arts and crafts to its captivating music and dance forms.

Discover the art of henna painting, an intricate form of body art that has been passed down through generations. Gain insights into the timeless Emirati traditions of falconry and camel racing, witnessing the deep-rooted connection between man and these magnificent creatures.

Embrace the mesmerizing sounds of traditional music, such as the soulful melodies of the oud or the rhythmic beats of the daf drum. Experience the captivating Emirati dances like the Ayyala, where performers clad in traditional attire sway in harmony, recounting tales of ancient tales and heroic deeds.

Immerse yourself in the vibrant souks, where the aroma of exotic spices fills the air and merchants proudly display their wares, from intricate carpets and handwoven textiles to dazzling gold and precious gemstones. Learn about the traditional art of Arabic calligraphy, a form of expression that beautifully intertwines language and art.

Emirati Culture and Heritage

Emirati Culture and Heritage in Dubai offer a captivating glimpse into the traditions and customs of the United Arab Emirates. Despite the city's modernity and cosmopolitan atmosphere, Dubai has remained deeply connected to its Emirati roots, preserving its rich cultural heritage for future generations to cherish and celebrate.

At the heart of Emirati culture is the value placed on hospitality and generosity. Emiratis are renowned for their warm welcome and genuine hospitality, inviting visitors to experience the essence of their culture firsthand. From traditional Arab coffee ceremonies to sharing a meal with locals, the Emirati hospitality is a memorable and authentic experience.

Emirati heritage is woven into every aspect of daily life, from traditional dress to culinary delights. The elegant attire of Emirati men, characterized by the crisp white kandura and the distinctive headpiece known as the ghutra, reflects the pride in their heritage. Women don the exquisite black abaya or vibrant traditional dresses, adorned with intricate embroidery and embellishments.

Emirati cuisine is a delicious blend of flavors and influences from the Arabian Peninsula and beyond. Indulge in dishes like machboos (a spiced rice dish), luqaimat (sweet dumplings), and camel meat specialties. Emirati cuisine is not only a treat for the taste buds but also a reflection of the country's history and cultural diversity.

Dubai is also home to numerous cultural attractions and festivals that celebrate Emirati heritage. The Sheikh Mohammed Centre for Cultural

Understanding offers immersive experiences, allowing visitors to engage with locals, learn about Emirati customs, and participate in traditional activities. The Dubai Heritage Village provides a glimpse into traditional Emirati life, showcasing traditional crafts, performances, and cultural exhibits.

Traditional Souks and Markets

Traditional Souks and Markets in Dubai offer a captivating journey into the bustling world of commerce and culture. Amidst the glitz and glamour of modern Dubai, these traditional marketplaces retain an authentic charm that harks back to the city's rich trading heritage.

One of the most iconic souks in Dubai is the Gold Souk, a dazzling showcase of the region's love for opulent jewelry. Stroll through the narrow alleyways adorned with countless shops glittering with gold and precious gemstones. From intricate necklaces to intricately designed bracelets, the Gold Souk is a treasure trove for those seeking exquisite jewelry pieces.

For a sensory delight, visit the Spice Souk, where vibrant colors and fragrant aromas fill the air. Explore the stalls brimming with a wide variety of spices, herbs, and traditional medicines. Let the aroma of cinnamon, saffron, and cardamom transport you to a world of culinary delights.

The Perfume Souk is a haven for those seeking unique scents and fragrances. Browse through a wide selection of perfumes, oils, and incense, often crafted with traditional methods passed down through generations. Discover captivating oriental fragrances that capture the essence of the Middle East.

Immerse yourself in the vibrant atmosphere of the Textile Souk, where an array of fabrics, silks, and textiles await. Admire the intricate embroidery and vibrant colors of traditional garments. From luxurious pashminas to delicate silk scarves, the Textile Souk offers a myriad of options for those seeking a touch of Middle Eastern elegance.

Emirati Cuisine and Dining Experiences

Emirati Cuisine and Dining Experiences in Dubai invite you on a mouthwatering journey through the flavors, aromas, and traditions of Emirati culinary heritage. Dubai, with its multicultural and cosmopolitan ambiance, offers a delightful blend of traditional Emirati dishes influenced by Bedouin, Arab, and Persian cuisines.

Emirati cuisine is a reflection of the region's history, heritage, and nomadic lifestyle. It combines simple yet flavorful ingredients to create dishes that are both comforting and satisfying. Indulge in dishes like machboos, a fragrant rice dish with tender meat or fish, flavored with aromatic spices. Savor the flavors of harees, a hearty dish made from wheat and slow-cooked meat, or try the flavorsome grilled meats like shawarma and kebabs.

Dining in Dubai provides an opportunity to experience the warm hospitality and generosity of Emirati culture. Traditional Emirati meals are often shared, emphasizing the importance of community and togetherness. Joining a Majlis, a traditional gathering, allows you to enjoy a feast of flavors while engaging in lively conversations.

While Dubai offers a wide range of international dining options, discovering Emirati cuisine is a must for a complete culinary experience. Visit local eateries and restaurants that specialize in Emirati fare, where you can relish authentic flavors and appreciate the culinary traditions that have shaped the region.

Beyond the flavors, Emirati dining experiences are enhanced by the ambiance and settings. Enjoy dining in Bedouin-style tents, where you can recline on comfortable cushions and savor a traditional meal under the starlit desert sky. For a modern twist, try Emirati fusion cuisine that combines traditional elements with contemporary techniques, creating innovative and exciting dishes.

Art and Design Scene in Dubai

The Art and Design Scene in Dubai is a vibrant and dynamic reflection of the city's cosmopolitan spirit and cultural diversity. From contemporary art galleries to innovative architectural marvels, Dubai has established itself as a hub for artistic expression and creativity.

The city boasts a flourishing art scene, with numerous galleries showcasing the works of both local and international artists. The Dubai Art

District, located in Al Quoz, is a thriving hub where art enthusiasts can explore a wide range of exhibitions, installations, and art events. From traditional paintings to avant-garde sculptures, the art scene in Dubai offers something for every artistic taste.

Dubai's skyline is a canvas itself, adorned with architectural marvels that push the boundaries of design and innovation. Iconic structures like the Burj Khalifa and the Burj Al Arab have become global symbols of architectural grandeur. The city's commitment to design excellence is evident in its futuristic skyscrapers, luxurious hotels, and awe-inspiring public spaces.

Design lovers will find inspiration in Dubai's numerous design festivals and events that celebrate creativity and innovation. The Dubai Design District (d3) is a dedicated hub that brings together designers, artists, and creative minds from around the world. Here, you can explore fashion boutiques, art galleries, and design studios, all contributing to the city's vibrant design landscape.

Dubai also hosts an array of art and design fairs, attracting international collectors and enthusiasts. The Dubai Design Week and Art Dubai are prominent events that showcase the best of contemporary art, design, and creative thinking.

CHAPTER 7: LUXURIOUS EXPERIENCES IN DUBAI

Luxurious Experiences in Dubai transport you to a world of opulence, indulgence, and lavishness. Renowned as a playground for the affluent, Dubai offers an array of upscale experiences that redefine luxury.

From extravagant hotels to high-end shopping destinations, Dubai's luxurious offerings are unmatched. Step into the world of luxury accommodations, where iconic hotels like the Burj Al Arab and Atlantis The Palm redefine the concept of indulgence. Enjoy lavish suites, private butlers, and breathtaking views that will leave you in awe.

Dubai is also home to some of the world's most prestigious shopping malls, such as The Dubai Mall and Mall of the Emirates. Explore luxury brands, haute couture boutiques, and exquisite jewelry stores, where you can indulge in the ultimate shopping experience.

For those seeking pampering and relaxation, Dubai's luxury spas and wellness centers offer a sanctuary of serenity. Immerse yourself in rejuvenating treatments, soothing massages, and exclusive wellness programs that will leave you feeling revitalized.

Fine dining is an essential part of the luxurious experience in Dubai. Indulge your palate in award-winning restaurants helmed by renowned chefs, offering a fusion of flavors from around the world. From elegant Michelin-starred establishments to rooftop dining with panoramic views, Dubai's culinary scene is a gastronomic delight.

Luxurious experiences in Dubai extend beyond the city's borders. Take a helicopter ride over the mesmerizing Palm Jumeirah or embark on a luxury yacht cruise along the coast, indulging in the ultimate maritime experience.

Dubai's commitment to providing unparalleled luxury experiences ensures that visitors are treated to a world of elegance, sophistication, and exclusivity. Whether you seek lavish accommodations, designer shopping, fine dining, or extraordinary experiences, Dubai promises to fulfill your desires and create memories that will last a lifetime.

Luxury Hotels and Resorts

The Burj Al Arab, often regarded as the epitome of luxury, stands tall as an iconic symbol of Dubai's hospitality. This sail-shaped masterpiece offers lavish suites, private butlers, and breathtaking views of the Arabian Gulf. It boasts a range of exceptional dining options, including the renowned Al Muntaha restaurant, situated on the 27th floor, offering panoramic views of the city.

Another prominent luxury hotel is Atlantis The Palm, located on the majestic Palm Jumeirah. This resort combines Arabian elegance with the thrill of an aquatic wonderland. Guests can enjoy spacious and luxurious rooms, dine at world-class restaurants, and explore the marine habitat of The Lost Chambers Aquarium or the exhilarating Aquaventure Waterpark.

The One&Only The Palm is a tranquil oasis nestled on the Palm Jumeirah's western crescent. It offers exclusive beachfront villas and impeccable service, where guests can indulge in personalized spa treatments, savor exquisite cuisine, and enjoy breathtaking views of the Dubai Marina skyline.

For those seeking a blend of luxury and cultural authenticity, the Jumeirah Al Qasr hotel is an ideal choice. Inspired by traditional Arabian palaces, this grand resort exudes elegance and charm. With its lush gardens, private beach, and authentic Arabian architecture, it provides a regal experience.

High-End Shopping in Dubai

The Dubai Mall, one of the world's largest shopping destinations, is a must-visit for luxury shoppers. With over 1,200 stores, it houses a collection of prestigious fashion brands, including Gucci, Chanel, Louis Vuitton, and Prada. The mall is a fashion haven, where visitors can explore the latest trends, shop for iconic designer pieces, and indulge in luxury shopping experiences.

Another renowned shopping destination is Mall of the Emirates, home to more than 700 high-end brands. Here, visitors can find luxury fashion labels, jewelry stores, and upscale boutiques. The mall is also famous for its Ski Dubai, an indoor ski resort that allows visitors to experience snow in the desert.

For those seeking a more exclusive shopping experience, The Avenue at Etihad Towers and City Walk offer an array of upscale boutiques and designer stores. These destinations provide a curated selection of luxury fashion, accessories, and beauty products, making them ideal for discerning shoppers looking for unique and rare finds.

Dubai's luxury shopping scene extends beyond malls and boutiques. The annual Dubai Shopping Festival and Dubai Summer Surprises are highly anticipated events that offer incredible discounts, promotions, and exclusive shopping experiences. During these festivals, visitors can enjoy fashion shows, live entertainment, and even win luxurious prizes.

Dubai's commitment to luxury shopping is further highlighted by its numerous luxury concept stores, such as Level Shoes and The Luxury Closet. These stores offer curated collections of designer footwear, handbags, and accessories, providing a seamless and immersive shopping experience.

In Dubai, high-end shopping is not just about purchasing luxury goods; it's a lifestyle experience that combines fashion, art, and entertainment. With its diverse retail landscape and unwavering dedication to luxury, Dubai is a true haven for those seeking the ultimate high-end shopping experience.

Exquisite Dining and Culinary Delights

Dubai is a culinary paradise that tantalizes the taste buds with its diverse and exquisite dining scene. From Michelin-starred restaurants to hidden gems tucked away in bustling neighborhoods, the city offers a gastronomic journey that caters to every palate and culinary preference.

Dubai is a melting pot of cultures, and its culinary landscape reflects this diversity. Visitors can savor authentic Emirati cuisine, which showcases traditional flavors and local ingredients. Signature dishes such as Machbous (spiced rice with meat or seafood) and Luqaimat (sweet dumplings) provide a delightful introduction to Emirati culinary traditions.

For those seeking international flavors, Dubai's dining scene offers an array of global cuisines prepared by world-class chefs. From gourmet French cuisine to Japanese delicacies, Indian spices to Italian classics, there is an endless variety of culinary delights to explore.

The city is also home to a vibrant street food culture, where food trucks and small eateries serve up a tantalizing mix of flavors from around the world. Visitors can indulge in shawarmas, falafels, and freshly grilled kebabs, immersing themselves in the vibrant street food atmosphere.

Dubai is known for its luxury dining experiences, with many restaurants boasting stunning views of the city skyline, the Arabian Gulf, or the desert landscape. Fine dining establishments like Pierchic and Nathan Outlaw at Al Mahara offer exceptional seafood experiences, while the renowned Atmosphere restaurant on the 122nd floor of the Burj Khalifa provides a dining experience at unparalleled heights.

In addition to its restaurants, Dubai is home to vibrant food markets and festivals that celebrate the city's culinary scene. The Dubai Food Festival, for example, is a much-anticipated event that showcases the best of local and international cuisine through food tastings, cooking demonstrations, and themed dining experiences.

For those seeking unique dining experiences, Dubai offers a range of options, including dining under the stars in the desert, enjoying a meal aboard a traditional dhow cruise, or indulging in a sumptuous brunch at one of the city's renowned hotels.

Spa and Wellness Retreats

Dubai is a haven of rejuvenation and relaxation, offering a wide range of luxurious spa and wellness retreats that cater to the needs of travelers seeking serenity and self-care. From world-class spa facilities to holistic wellness programs, the city provides an oasis of tranquility amidst its vibrant energy.

Dubai's luxury hotels and resorts boast opulent spas that offer a variety of treatments inspired by ancient healing traditions from around the world. Visitors can indulge in rejuvenating massages, invigorating body scrubs, and revitalizing facials, all performed by skilled therapists in serene and lavish surroundings.

Wellness retreats in Dubai go beyond traditional spa experiences, offering comprehensive programs focused on holistic wellbeing. These retreats provide personalized fitness sessions, wellness consultations, yoga and meditation classes, and nutritious culinary experiences. The serene desert landscapes and breathtaking beachfront settings add to the overall tranquility and serenity of these retreats.

Many wellness retreats in Dubai also incorporate traditional healing practices, such as Ayurveda and Traditional Chinese Medicine, into their programs. These ancient therapies help restore balance and promote overall wellness, allowing guests to embark on a transformative journey of self-discovery and healing.

The city is also home to state-of-the-art wellness centers that offer cutting-edge treatments and advanced wellness technologies. Cryotherapy, hydrotherapy, and sound therapy are just a few examples of the innovative therapies available to enhance physical and mental wellbeing.

Dubai's wellness scene extends beyond spas and retreats. The city is dotted with lush parks, tranquil beaches, and scenic jogging tracks, providing ample opportunities for outdoor activities and exercise. Fitness enthusiasts can enjoy a range of options, from beachfront yoga classes to high-intensity interval training sessions.

CHAPTER 8: THRILLING ADVENTURE AND OUTDOOR ACTIVITIES

Dubai is not just a city of skyscrapers and luxury, but also a playground for thrilling adventure and outdoor activities. From desert adventures to water sports, the city offers a myriad of opportunities for adrenaline junkies and outdoor enthusiasts.

One of the most popular activities in Dubai is dune bashing, where visitors can hop into a 4x4 vehicle and explore the magnificent sand dunes of the Arabian Desert. Experienced drivers navigate through the undulating terrain, creating an exhilarating experience filled with adrenaline and excitement.

For those seeking a more traditional desert experience, camel riding and sandboarding are fantastic options. Riding a camel through the vast desert landscapes allows visitors to soak in the beauty of the surroundings while enjoying a gentle and traditional mode of transportation. Sandboarding, on the other hand, offers a thrilling ride down the sandy slopes, reminiscent of snowboarding.

Dubai's coastal location also provides ample opportunities for water sports and aquatic adventures. Visitors can engage in jet skiing, flyboarding, parasailing, and even skydiving over the breathtaking Palm Jumeirah. The warm waters of the Arabian Gulf are perfect for diving and snorkeling, allowing enthusiasts to explore vibrant coral reefs and encounter marine life.

For a unique adventure, visitors can take a seaplane tour and enjoy stunning aerial views of Dubai's iconic landmarks, including the Burj Khalifa and the Palm Jumeirah. This unforgettable experience combines the thrill of flying with the beauty of the cityscape.

Dubai is also home to a variety of theme parks and outdoor adventure parks. From the thrilling roller coasters of Dubai Parks and Resorts to the zip lines and obstacle courses of Aventura Park, there are plenty of options for family-friendly fun and excitement.

Additionally, Dubai offers golf courses, tennis courts, and cycling tracks for those who enjoy more leisurely outdoor activities. The city's commitment to providing well-maintained parks and green spaces allows visitors and residents to enjoy picnics, jogging, and leisurely strolls.

Desert Safaris and Dune Bashing

One of the most thrilling and iconic experiences you can have is embarking on a desert safari and dune bashing adventure. This exhilarating activity allows you to immerse yourself in the beauty of the desert while enjoying an adrenaline-fueled ride through the sandy terrain.

Desert safaris typically begin with a comfortable and scenic drive from the city to the outskirts, where the expansive desert awaits. Upon arrival, expert drivers guide you through the mesmerizing sand dunes in a 4x4 vehicle, creating a heart-pounding experience that combines speed, skill, and breathtaking views. The sensation of gliding over the dunes, with the sand swirling around you, is truly an unforgettable experience.

As you traverse the dunes, your skilled driver will navigate the rugged terrain, taking you on a thrilling rollercoaster-like adventure. The vehicle twists and turns, surging up and down the steep dunes, providing a rush of adrenaline and excitement. The beauty of the desert unfolds before your eyes, with endless golden sands stretching as far as the eye can see.

During a desert safari, you'll also have the opportunity to engage in other activities that showcase the unique charm of the desert. Camel riding allows you to experience the traditional mode of transport in the region, as you gently sway atop these magnificent creatures, traversing the desert landscape.

Another highlight of a desert safari is sandboarding, where you can strap on a board and glide down the slopes of the dunes, much like snowboarding. It's a thrilling and exhilarating experience, as you navigate the sandy terrain and feel the rush of adrenaline.

To top off your desert safari, you'll be treated to a traditional Bedouin-style camp where you can relax and unwind. Here, you can indulge in a sumptuous barbecue dinner, savoring mouthwatering local delicacies while being entertained by mesmerizing performances such as belly dancing and Tanoura shows. You can also get henna tattoos, enjoy a shisha session, and witness a stunning sunset in the tranquil desert setting.

Water Sports: Jet Skiing, Parasailing, and more

One of the most popular water sports in Dubai is jet skiing. Renting a jet ski allows you to experience the thrill of gliding across the azure waters, feeling the wind in your hair as you navigate the waves. You can explore the coastline, enjoy panoramic views of Dubai's iconic landmarks, and even challenge yourself with some high-speed maneuvers.

For those looking for a unique perspective, parasailing offers a breathtaking aerial adventure. Suspended from a parachute, you'll be lifted into the sky, soaring above the water and taking in the panoramic views of the city's skyline and coastline. It's an exhilarating experience that combines the thrill of flying with the tranquility of being out on the water.

Dubai is also a popular destination for wakeboarding and water skiing. Skimming across the water's surface, propelled by the speedboat, you can showcase your skills and perform tricks or simply enjoy the rush of adrenaline as you carve through the waves. Lessons and equipment rentals are readily available, making it accessible to both beginners and experienced enthusiasts.

Another exciting water sport in Dubai is flyboarding. Strap on a jetpack-like device that propels you above the water's surface, allowing you to hover, dive, and perform acrobatic maneuvers. It's a thrilling and unique experience that will make you feel like a superhero as you defy gravity.

If you're looking for a more leisurely water activity, kayaking and paddleboarding are great options. Explore the tranquil waterways, paddle through mangrove forests, or simply enjoy a relaxing ride along the coastline. It's an excellent way to connect with nature and enjoy the serene beauty of Dubai's coastal environment.

Dubai's warm waters also offer fantastic opportunities for snorkeling and scuba diving. Dive beneath the surface and discover vibrant coral reefs teeming with marine life. Whether you're a certified diver or a beginner looking to try diving for the first time, Dubai's dive centers and dive sites cater to all levels of experience.

Skydiving over Palm Jumeirah

Skydiving over Palm Jumeirah in Dubai is a once-in-a-lifetime experience that combines the thrill of freefalling with breathtaking views of one of the city's most iconic landmarks. Imagine soaring through the sky, feeling the rush of adrenaline as you descend from an aircraft and witness the awe-inspiring beauty of the palm-shaped island from above.

The adventure begins at a state-of-the-art skydiving center, where you'll receive a safety briefing and be equipped with a jumpsuit, harness, and all necessary gear. Experienced instructors will guide you through the entire process, ensuring your safety and providing expert guidance throughout the jump.

As you ascend to altitude in the aircraft, your excitement and anticipation build. The doors open, and it's time to take the leap. With the instructor securely attached to you, you step out into the open sky, and the exhilarating freefall begins. The sensation of rushing through the air, feeling the wind on your face, and the adrenaline pumping through your veins is simply indescribable.

As you freefall, the expansive view of Palm Jumeirah unfolds beneath you. The man-made archipelago, with its palm tree-shaped layout and luxurious resorts, stretches out like a work of art against the backdrop of the sparkling Arabian Gulf. The aerial perspective offers a unique and awe-inspiring vantage point that few get to experience.

After an exhilarating freefall, the parachute is deployed, and you transition into a peaceful canopy ride. From this height, you can fully appreciate the beauty of Palm Jumeirah and its surroundings. The view of the pristine beaches, turquoise waters, and the stunning Dubai skyline in the distance is nothing short of breathtaking.

As you gently descend towards the landing zone, the excitement and sense of accomplishment fill your being. Touching down on the ground, you'll be overwhelmed with a sense of achievement and the realization that you've just experienced something truly extraordinary.

Theme Parks and Entertainment

One of the most famous theme parks in Dubai is Dubai Parks and Resorts, an expansive entertainment complex that houses several parks, including Motiongate Dubai, Bollywood Parks Dubai, and Legoland Dubai. Motiongate Dubai brings the magic of Hollywood to life, with rides and attractions inspired by popular movies and characters. Bollywood Parks Dubai celebrates the vibrant world of Indian cinema, offering live shows, musicals, and interactive experiences. Legoland Dubai is a paradise for families, with its colorful Lego-themed attractions, rides, and building experiences that inspire creativity and imagination.

For adrenaline junkies, IMG Worlds of Adventure is the place to be. As the world's largest indoor theme park, it offers an array of exhilarating rides and experiences based on popular franchises like

Marvel, Cartoon Network, and more. From high-speed roller coasters to immersive 3D attractions, there's no shortage of heart-pounding excitement at IMG Worlds of Adventure.

Dubai also boasts the world-famous Aquaventure Waterpark, located at Atlantis, The Palm. This aquatic playground features thrilling water slides, a lazy river, a wave pool, and a private beach, providing hours of wet and wild fun for the whole family. The park's star attraction is the Leap of Faith slide, which sends brave riders plummeting through a clear tunnel surrounded by shark-infested waters.

If you're looking for an entertainment experience that combines excitement with cultural immersion, Global Village is a must-visit. This seasonal cultural and entertainment extravaganza showcases pavilions from different countries, offering a glimpse into their traditions, cuisine, and arts. With live performances, thrilling rides, and a bustling market, Global Village is a vibrant celebration of diversity and global cultures.

Dubai's theme parks and entertainment options are not limited to the aforementioned attractions. From indoor skiing at Ski Dubai to the adrenaline-pumping rides at Ferrari World Abu Dhabi, there's always something new and thrilling to discover in this entertainment hub of the Middle East.

CHAPTER 9: UNDERSTANDING FOREIGN TRANSACTION FEES

Understanding foreign transaction fees is crucial when traveling to Dubai or any other international destination. Foreign transaction fees are charges imposed by credit card companies or banks for converting your currency during a purchase or withdrawal made abroad.

When using your credit card in Dubai, especially for shopping, dining, or other transactions, it's important to be aware of any foreign transaction fees that may apply. These fees can vary from one card issuer to another, so it's advisable to check with your bank or credit card provider before your trip.

Foreign transaction fees typically consist of two components: a currency conversion fee and an international transaction fee. The currency conversion fee is a percentage charged for converting your local currency to the UAE Dirham (AED). This fee is often around 1-3% of the transaction amount. The international transaction fee, on the other hand, is a flat fee charged for making a purchase in a foreign country. It is usually around 1-3% of the transaction amount as well.

To avoid or minimize foreign transaction fees in Dubai, consider the following tips:

- Inform your bank or credit card company about your travel plans to Dubai in advance. This helps them monitor and authorize your transactions to prevent any unnecessary declines or security concerns.

- Consider using a credit card that offers no foreign transaction fees. Some credit card issuers provide cards specifically designed for international travelers, with no additional fees for purchases made abroad.

- Opt for cash payments in local currency when possible. By using cash, you avoid the currency conversion fees associated with credit card transactions.

- Use ATMs wisely. When withdrawing cash from ATMs in Dubai, be aware that your bank may charge a foreign ATM withdrawal fee in addition to any currency conversion fees.

Avoid Cell Phone Roaming Charges

Avoiding cell phone roaming charges is essential when traveling to Dubai to ensure you don't face exorbitant fees for using your mobile device. Here are some tips to help you avoid roaming charges and stay connected without breaking the bank.

Check with your mobile service provider: Before your trip, contact your mobile service provider to understand their international roaming policies and packages. They may offer temporary international plans or data packages specifically for travelers to Dubai.

Activate airplane mode and use Wi-Fi: To prevent accidental roaming, activate airplane mode on your device. Then, connect to Wi-Fi networks available in hotels, cafes, and public areas. This allows you to use messaging apps, make internet calls, and access online services without incurring roaming charges.

Use local SIM cards: Consider purchasing a local SIM card upon arrival in Dubai. This allows you to have a local phone number and access to local rates for calls, texts, and data. Make sure your phone is unlocked and compatible with the local network.

Utilize messaging and calling apps: Take advantage of messaging apps such as WhatsApp, Skype, or Viber to stay in touch with family and friends. These apps use data or Wi-Fi connections, minimizing the need for cellular calls and texts.

Download offline maps and guides: Before your trip, download offline maps and travel guides to your mobile device. This way, you can navigate Dubai without relying on data or GPS, saving on roaming charges.

Enable data-saving settings: Adjust your device's settings to reduce data usage. Disable automatic app updates, limit background data usage, and use data-saving modes available on most smartphones.

Consider a Dubai SIM Card or Mifi Device

Consider getting a Dubai SIM card or a portable Wi-Fi device (MiFi) to stay connected and avoid high roaming charges during your visit to Dubai. These options provide local connectivity and can be a cost-effective solution for staying connected to the internet and making calls.

A Dubai SIM card can be easily purchased upon arrival at the airport or from various retail outlets throughout the city. Simply insert the SIM card into your unlocked phone, and you'll have access to a local phone number and data plan. This allows you to make local calls, send texts, and use data at affordable local rates. You can choose from different data packages based on your needs and duration of stay.

Alternatively, you can opt for a portable Wi-Fi device, also known as a MiFi device. These devices provide a mobile hotspot that you can connect to with your smartphone, tablet, or laptop. MiFi devices are convenient for travelers as they allow multiple devices to connect simultaneously, and you can easily share the device with your travel companions. You can either rent a MiFi device or purchase one, depending on your preference.

By using a Dubai SIM card or a MiFi device, you can enjoy uninterrupted internet access, make local calls, and stay connected with your loved ones throughout your stay. It gives you the flexibility and convenience of having a reliable internet connection wherever you go in Dubai, without the worry of excessive roaming charges.

Consider The Adapter and Converter

When traveling to Dubai, it's important to consider the need for adapters and converters to ensure your electronic devices can be used safely and efficiently. Dubai, like many other countries, has its own electrical standards and plug types that may differ from what you're used to in your home country.

Dubai uses the British-style three-pin plug (Type G), which has three rectangular pins in a triangular pattern. If your devices have plugs that are not compatible with this type, you will need an adapter. Adapters are relatively inexpensive and readily available at airports, electronic stores, and online retailers. They allow you to plug your devices into Dubai's electrical outlets.

In addition to adapters, you may also need a voltage converter or transformer. Dubai operates on a 220-240V electrical system, while some countries use a different voltage (e.g., 110-120V). If your device is not compatible with the higher voltage used in Dubai, you will need a converter to avoid damage to your electronics. It's important to note that many modern electronic devices, such as smartphones and laptops, are designed to handle a wide range of voltages. Check the voltage rating on your device or consult the manufacturer's specifications to determine if a converter is necessary.

Consider Buying An Adapter or SIM Card

It's important to consider purchasing an adapter or a SIM card to enhance your travel experience and stay connected. These items can greatly contribute to your convenience and communication while exploring the city.

Firstly, investing in an adapter is crucial for using your electronic devices in Dubai. The electrical outlets in Dubai typically follow the British-style three-pin plug (Type G) configuration. If your devices have different plug types, purchasing an adapter will allow you to easily plug them into the local outlets. Adapters are widely available in airports, electronic stores, and online retailers, ensuring you can find the right one for your needs.

Secondly, acquiring a local SIM card can greatly enhance your connectivity during your stay in Dubai. By purchasing a Dubai SIM card, you'll have access to a local phone number and data plan, enabling you to make local calls, send texts, and use mobile data at affordable rates. This allows you to stay connected with your travel companions, access online maps, and communicate with locals and tourist services more conveniently.

Before your trip, research different telecom providers in Dubai to find the most suitable SIM card options based on your data and call needs. You can purchase SIM cards at airports, shopping malls, and telecom provider stores. Be sure to check if your phone is unlocked and compatible with the local network frequencies.

Download Offline Map

When traveling to Dubai, it's highly recommended to download offline maps to your smartphone or tablet. Having an offline map can be incredibly useful in navigating the city, especially if you don't have access to a constant internet connection or if you want to avoid excessive data charges.

By downloading an offline map, you'll have access to detailed street maps, landmarks, and points of interest without relying on a live internet connection. You can easily plan your routes, find nearby attractions, and navigate through Dubai's streets confidently.

Several popular mapping applications, such as Google Maps and Maps.me, offer the option to download offline maps for specific regions or cities. These maps typically include key information like street names, locations of hotels, restaurants, shopping malls, and other points of interest. You can choose the map area you want to download and save it to your device before your trip.

Downloading an offline map can also be beneficial for saving battery life since your device won't continuously use data or rely on GPS signals. It provides a convenient and reliable navigation tool even in areas with weak or no internet connectivity.

Before your trip, make sure to download the desired offline maps while you have an internet connection. Remember to periodically update the offline map to ensure you have the most accurate and up-to-date information during your stay.

Cash and Credit Card

When it comes to managing your finances in Dubai, it's essential to consider both cash and credit cards for your transactions. Understanding how to use and access cash and credit cards will ensure a smooth and hassle-free experience during your visit.

Dubai is a modern city with a well-developed banking system, and credit cards are widely accepted in most establishments, including hotels, restaurants, and shops. Using a credit card offers convenience and security, as you don't need to carry large amounts of cash with you. Major credit cards like Visa and Mastercard are commonly accepted, but it's always wise to carry multiple cards from different issuers in case one is not accepted.

However, it's important to have some cash on hand for small expenses, especially in local markets, smaller shops, and street vendors where credit cards may not be accepted. Many ATMs are available throughout the city, allowing you to withdraw cash in the local currency, Emirati Dirham (AED). Be aware that some ATMs may charge withdrawal fees, so it's advisable to check with your bank regarding any foreign transaction fees or currency conversion charges that may apply.

It's also worth noting that some establishments, particularly smaller businesses or street vendors, may prefer cash transactions. Keeping smaller denomination notes can be helpful for convenience.

Regardless of whether you use cash or credit cards, it's important to keep an eye on your spending and regularly check your account statements for any unauthorized transactions. It's also advisable to inform your bank or credit card provider about your travel plans to avoid any potential card blocks due to suspicious activity.

Cash at the Airport is Expensive

If you're planning to exchange currency or obtain cash upon arrival at the airport in Dubai, it's important to be aware that the rates and fees at airport currency exchange counters can be quite expensive compared to other options. It's generally recommended to avoid exchanging large amounts of cash at the airport and consider alternative methods for obtaining local currency.

Airport currency exchange counters often charge higher exchange rates and additional fees, which can significantly reduce the value of your money. These rates are typically less favorable compared to those offered by local banks or currency exchange offices in the city.

To get the best exchange rates and reduce fees, consider exchanging a small amount of cash for immediate expenses, such as transportation or small purchases, and then seek out alternative options in the city. Local banks or authorized currency exchange offices in Dubai generally offer more competitive rates and lower fees. It's advisable to compare rates from different sources to find the best deal.

Alternatively, you can also withdraw cash from ATMs in Dubai using your debit or credit card. This option often provides a more favorable exchange rate compared to airport currency exchange counters. However, be aware that some banks may charge foreign transaction fees or ATM withdrawal fees, so it's important to check with your bank beforehand to understand any potential charges.

Why Cash May Not Work

Dubai is a modern city that heavily relies on electronic payment systems, and while cash is generally accepted, there are several reasons why it may not be the most convenient option.

Firstly, many establishments in Dubai, including hotels, restaurants, and shops, prefer electronic payment methods such as credit cards or mobile payment apps. This is especially true for larger, more upscale establishments. Carrying and using cash may limit your options when it comes to making purchases or paying for services.

Secondly, Dubai is a popular tourist destination attracting visitors from around the world. As a result, it's not uncommon to encounter counterfeit currency. To combat this issue, many businesses in Dubai exercise caution when accepting cash, leading them to rely more on electronic payment methods for security and ease of transaction.

Moreover, carrying large amounts of cash can be a safety concern. While Dubai is generally a safe city, it's always wise to take precautions and minimize the risk of theft or loss. By relying on electronic payment methods, you can avoid the need to carry excessive amounts of cash with you.

Lastly, Dubai's currency, the Emirati Dirham (AED), may not be readily available or easily exchangeable in your home country. This can make it challenging to obtain or exchange cash in advance, making electronic payment methods a more practical choice.

Set up Apple pay or Google pay as an Option

Setting up Apple Pay or Google Pay as a payment option in Dubai can greatly enhance your convenience and efficiency during your stay. These mobile payment systems offer a seamless and secure way to make transactions, allowing you to leave your physical wallet behind and rely on your smartphone instead.

Both Apple Pay and Google Pay are widely accepted in Dubai, with many establishments equipped with contactless payment terminals. To set up Apple Pay, simply add your eligible credit or debit card to the Wallet app on your iPhone or Apple Watch. For Google Pay, you can add your cards to the Google Pay app on your Android device.

By using Apple Pay or Google Pay, you eliminate the need to carry physical cash or credit cards, reducing the risk of loss or theft. These payment systems utilize tokenization technology, which replaces your card details with a unique identifier, ensuring that your payment information remains secure and protected.

In Dubai, you'll find that most retail stores, restaurants, and entertainment venues accept contactless payments, making Apple Pay or Google Pay a convenient option for quick and hassle-free transactions. Simply hold your device near the payment terminal and authenticate the transaction with your fingerprint, Face ID, or passcode.

Another advantage of using mobile payment systems is the ability to store digital versions of loyalty cards, tickets, and boarding passes, reducing the clutter in your physical wallet and providing easy access to these important documents.

CHAPTER 10: INSIDER TIPS AND LOCAL SECRETS

Unlocking the hidden gems and insider secrets of Dubai can elevate your travel experience and introduce you to unique aspects of the city that are often missed by tourists. With insider tips and local secrets, you'll discover the true essence of Dubai and make the most of your time in this captivating destination.

Locals in Dubai have an intimate knowledge of the city, its culture, and its hidden treasures. They can provide invaluable insights and recommendations that may not be found in mainstream tourist guides. From lesser-known attractions and off-the-beaten-path neighborhoods to authentic local eateries and hidden boutiques, these insider tips will allow you to delve deeper into Dubai's vibrant tapestry.

Embracing the guidance of locals can also enhance your understanding of the local customs and traditions, ensuring you navigate the city with respect and cultural sensitivity. They can advise on appropriate attire, local etiquette, and the best times to visit popular sites to avoid crowds.

Moreover, insider tips can help you navigate Dubai's transportation system, providing insights on the most efficient ways to get around the city. From knowing which metro line to take for a specific attraction to utilizing local transportation apps for seamless navigation, these tips will save you time and enhance your overall travel experience.

Additionally, insiders can shed light on unique experiences and events happening during your visit. They may inform you about local festivals, art exhibitions, or hidden live music venues that offer a glimpse into the vibrant cultural scene of Dubai.

Hidden Gems and Off-the-Beaten-Path Experiences

While Dubai is known for its iconic landmarks and bustling cityscape, the city also boasts a wealth of hidden gems and off-the-beaten-path experiences that offer a different perspective on this dynamic destination. Exploring these lesser-known treasures will allow you to discover a side of Dubai that many tourists overlook.

One such hidden gem is Al Fahidi Historical Neighbourhood, a charming district that offers a glimpse into Dubai's past. With its narrow winding lanes, traditional wind towers, and historic buildings, this area transports you back in time to the city's early days. Explore the Al Fahidi Fort, home to the Dubai Museum, and immerse yourself in the rich heritage and culture of the region.

For nature lovers, a visit to Ras Al Khor Wildlife Sanctuary is a must. This protected area is home to a variety of bird species, including flamingos, herons, and eagles. Take a walk along the boardwalks and observe the birds in their natural habitat, offering a serene and peaceful escape from the city's hustle and bustle.

Escape the city's glitz and glamour and head to the Hatta Mountains. Located just outside of Dubai, this mountainous region offers stunning landscapes, including rugged terrains, gushing waterfalls, and picturesque hiking trails. Explore the Hatta Heritage Village, visit the Hatta Dam, or enjoy thrilling activities such as mountain biking or kayaking.

To experience Dubai's thriving art scene, visit Alserkal Avenue, a vibrant arts district that is home to numerous contemporary art galleries, creative spaces, and cultural events. Discover local and international art exhibitions, attend workshops, and immerse yourself in the city's artistic expression.

Dos and Don'ts in Dubai

As you explore the city's attractions and immerse yourself in its unique culture, it is important to be aware of the dos and don'ts to ensure a respectful and enjoyable experience. Here is a comprehensive guide to help you navigate the social norms and cultural etiquette of Dubai.

Dos:

1. Dress modestly: Dubai follows a conservative dress code, especially in public areas. It is advisable to dress modestly, covering your shoulders, knees, and cleavage. While swimwear is acceptable at beaches and pools, it is best to wear a cover-up when walking to and from these areas.

2. Respect Islamic traditions: Dubai is an Islamic city, and it is important to respect local customs and traditions. During the holy month of Ramadan, refrain from eating, drinking, or smoking in public during daylight hours. Dress appropriately and be mindful of prayer times, as mosques may be busy during these periods.

3. Greet with respect: When meeting locals or business associates, it is customary to greet with a handshake and a polite greeting such as "As-salamu alaykum" (peace be upon you). Use appropriate titles such as Mr., Mrs., or Sheikh when addressing individuals, unless otherwise instructed.

4. Follow cultural norms: Dubai values politeness and respect. Be courteous to others, avoid public displays of affection, and refrain from using offensive language or gestures. Accept offers of Arabic coffee or tea as a sign of hospitality, and use your right hand for eating, greeting, and handing over items.

5. Observe local laws and regulations: Dubai has strict laws, and it is essential to familiarize yourself with them. Respect traffic rules, avoid public intoxication, and be mindful of photography restrictions, especially near government buildings and military installations.

Don'ts:

1. Public displays of affection: Dubai has conservative values, and public displays of affection, such as kissing or hugging in public, are considered inappropriate. Keep expressions of affection private to avoid offending local sensibilities.

2. Offensive behavior or language: Dubai is a multicultural city, and it is essential to be respectful and tolerant of different cultures and beliefs. Avoid making derogatory or offensive remarks about any religion, culture, or individual.

3. Alcohol consumption in public: While alcohol is served in licensed establishments

such as hotels and restaurants, consuming alcohol in public areas or being intoxicated in public is strictly prohibited. Be mindful of your alcohol consumption and enjoy it responsibly.

4. Disrespectful attire: Avoid wearing revealing or provocative clothing, especially in public places. This includes clothing that displays offensive language or symbols. Dress appropriately, respecting local customs and cultural sensitivities.

5. Photography without permission: It is important to respect people's privacy and seek permission before taking photographs, especially of individuals or religious sites. Some areas, such as military installations, may have strict photography restrictions, so be aware of your surroundings and follow any signage or instructions.

6. Disrespecting Ramadan: During the holy month of Ramadan, it is important to be respectful and observant of fasting hours. Avoid eating, drinking, or smoking in public

during daylight hours out of consideration for those who are fasting.

7. Engaging in illegal activities: Dubai has strict laws regarding drug use, possession, and trafficking. Engaging in any illegal activities can result in severe penalties and legal consequences. Familiarize yourself with local laws and abide by them at all times.

Useful Phrases and Language Tips

While English is widely spoken in Dubai, locals appreciate visitors who make an effort to learn a few basic Arabic phrases. Here are some useful phrases and language tips to enhance your communication and cultural experience in Dubai:

Greetings:
- Hello: Marhaba
- Good morning: Sabah al khair
- Good evening: Masaa' al khair
- Thank you: Shukran
- Please: Min fadlak (to a male), Min fadlik (to a female)

Polite Expressions:

- Excuse me: Samahani
- Sorry: Asif
- Yes: Naam
- No: Laa
- I don't understand: Ana laa afham

Basic Numbers:

- One: Wahid
- Two: Ethnain
- Three: Thalatha
- Ten: Ashara

Ordering Food and Drinks:

- I would like...: Oreed...
- Water: Ma'
- Coffee: Qahwa
- Tea: Shay

Getting Directions:

- Where is...?: Ayna...?
- Left: Yasar
- Right: Yameen
- Straight ahead: Ala tool

Cultural Etiquette:

- It is customary to greet with a handshake and a smile.
- Address older individuals and those in positions of authority with respect.
- When visiting mosques, dress modestly and remove your shoes before entering.
- It is polite to accept offers of Arabic coffee or tea as a sign of hospitality.

Language Tips:

- Learn some basic Arabic phrases before your trip to show your interest and respect for the local culture.
- Practice your pronunciation by listening to native speakers or using language learning apps.
- Be patient and understanding if you encounter language barriers. Many people in Dubai are multilingual and will try their best to communicate with you.

CHAPTER 11: PRACTICAL INFORMATION

When traveling to Dubai, it's essential to have some practical information at your fingertips to ensure a smooth and enjoyable experience. Here are some key details to keep in mind:

Time Zone: Dubai operates on Gulf Standard Time (GST), which is UTC+4.

Currency: The official currency of Dubai is the UAE Dirham (AED). It's advisable to carry some local currency for small purchases, but credit cards are widely accepted in most establishments.

Weather: Dubai has a desert climate, characterized by hot summers and mild winters. The summer months (June to September) can be scorching, with temperatures reaching up to 45°C (113°F). Winter (November to February) offers more pleasant temperatures, ranging from 15°C to 25°C (59°F to 77°F).

Dress Code: While Dubai is relatively liberal, it's important to respect local customs and dress modestly, especially in public places and religious sites. When visiting mosques, women are expected to cover their shoulders and knees, and men should wear long pants.

Transportation: Dubai has an extensive public transportation system, including the Dubai Metro, buses, and taxis. The metro is a convenient way to get around the city, and taxis are readily available. Ride-hailing services like Uber and Careem are also popular.

Electricity: Dubai operates on a 220-240V electrical system. The standard power plugs are of the three-pin type, so it's advisable to bring a universal adapter if your devices have a different plug type.

Safety: Dubai is generally considered a safe city for travelers. However, it's always wise to take standard precautions, such as keeping an eye on your belongings, avoiding isolated areas at night, and following local laws and regulations.

Language: The official language of Dubai is Arabic, but English is widely spoken and understood, especially in tourist areas and major establishments.

Emergency Numbers: In case of emergencies, dial 999 for police, 998 for ambulance services, and 997 for the fire department.

Health and Safety Tips

Stay Hydrated: Dubai's climate can be hot and dry, especially during the summer months. Drink plenty of water to stay hydrated throughout the day, especially if you're spending time outdoors.

Sun Protection: The sun in Dubai can be intense, so it's crucial to protect yourself from harmful UV rays. Wear sunscreen with a high SPF, a wide-brimmed hat, sunglasses, and lightweight, breathable clothing.

Respect Local Customs: Dubai is a culturally diverse city with a mix of traditions and customs. Respect the local culture by dressing modestly in public places, particularly in religious sites, and be mindful of local customs and traditions.

Food and Water Safety: Dubai has a wide range of dining options, but it's important to exercise caution when it comes to food and water. Stick to reputable restaurants and establishments that maintain high hygiene standards. Drink bottled water or use filtered water for drinking and brushing your teeth.

Medical Facilities: Dubai boasts excellent medical facilities and hospitals. If you require medical assistance, don't hesitate to seek help. It's recommended to have travel insurance that covers any medical emergencies during your trip.

COVID-19 Precautions: In light of the ongoing pandemic, it's essential to stay informed about the latest COVID-19 guidelines and adhere to them. Follow social distancing measures, wear a mask in public places, and sanitize your hands regularly.

Road Safety: Dubai has a well-developed road infrastructure, but it's important to practice caution when crossing roads and obey traffic rules. If you plan to drive, ensure you have a valid international driving permit and familiarize yourself with local driving regulations.

Travel Insurance: It's highly recommended to have comprehensive travel insurance that covers medical emergencies, trip cancellations, and lost belongings.

This will provide you with peace of mind and financial protection during your trip.

Transportation Options and Public Transport
Dubai offers a variety of transportation options to help you navigate the city with ease. Whether you're traveling within the city or exploring its outskirts, here are some key transportation options and public transport tips to keep in mind:

Dubai Metro: The Dubai Metro is a modern and efficient way to get around the city. It has two lines, the Red Line and the Green Line, which connect major attractions, business districts, and residential areas. The metro operates from early morning until midnight on weekdays and until 1 am on weekends.

Public Buses: Dubai has an extensive bus network that covers various routes across the city. The buses are air-conditioned, comfortable, and offer an affordable way to travel. They operate from early morning until midnight, and some routes even run 24 hours.

Taxis: Taxis are a popular mode of transportation in Dubai. They are readily available and easily identifiable with their distinctive cream color and rooftop signs. Taxis are metered, and it's advisable to use licensed taxis for a safe and reliable journey.

Tram: The Dubai Tram serves areas in the Dubai Marina and Jumeirah Beach Residence (JBR) area. It offers convenient access to popular destinations along the tram route, including shopping malls, hotels, and entertainment venues.

Ride-Hailing Apps: Uber and Careem are widely used ride-hailing apps in Dubai. They provide a convenient and reliable way to book private cars for transportation.

Water Taxis and Abras: For a unique transportation experience, you can take a water taxi or abra, which are traditional wooden boats, across Dubai Creek. They offer a scenic and traditional way to travel between Deira and Bur Dubai.

Nol Card: The Nol Card is a smart card used for payment across various modes of public transport in Dubai, including the metro, buses, trams, and water buses. It's recommended to get a Nol Card for seamless travel and fare integration.

Internet and Connectivity

Staying connected and having reliable internet access is essential for travelers, and Dubai offers excellent connectivity options to meet these needs. Here's what you need to know about internet and connectivity in Dubai:

Mobile Data: Dubai has excellent mobile network coverage, and you can easily purchase a local SIM card upon arrival at the airport or from various mobile service providers across the city. These SIM cards offer data packages that cater to different needs, allowing you to stay connected on the go.

Wi-Fi Hotspots: Dubai is well-equipped with Wi-Fi hotspots, and many hotels, restaurants, cafes, and public spaces provide free Wi-Fi access to their customers. Additionally, the Dubai Metro, Dubai Tram, and some public parks offer Wi-Fi connectivity, making it convenient to stay connected while exploring the city.

Internet Cafes: If you don't have a device or need to use a computer with internet access, you can find internet cafes in Dubai. These cafes typically charge an hourly rate for internet usage and have facilities such as computers, printers, and scanners.

Roaming Services: If you prefer to use your own mobile plan from your home country, it's advisable to check with your mobile service provider regarding international roaming options and costs in Dubai. Keep in mind that roaming charges can be expensive, so it's recommended to compare rates and consider alternative options such as purchasing a local SIM card.

Public Wi-Fi Zones: The Dubai government has implemented free public Wi-Fi zones in several areas across the city, including parks, beaches, and popular tourist attractions. These zones provide visitors with complimentary internet access and are indicated by signage in the respective locations.

Accommodation Recommendations

Dubai offers a wide range of accommodation options to suit every traveler's preferences and budget. Whether you're looking for luxury hotels, cozy boutique stays, or budget-friendly accommodations, here are some recommendations to help you choose the perfect place to stay in Dubai:

1. Luxury Hotels: Dubai is renowned for its luxurious hotels that provide world-class amenities and exceptional service. From iconic hotels like Burj Al Arab and Atlantis, The Palm to renowned chains such as Jumeirah, Ritz-Carlton, and Four Seasons, these properties offer opulent accommodations, stunning views, and unparalleled comfort.

2. Beachfront Resorts: If you want to enjoy Dubai's beautiful coastline, consider staying at one of the beachfront resorts. Hotels along Jumeirah Beach Residence (JBR) or Palm Jumeirah provide direct access to pristine beaches, along with a range of facilities such as pools, spas, and beachfront dining options.

3. Downtown Dubai: For those seeking a vibrant urban experience, Downtown Dubai is an excellent choice. This area is home to the iconic Burj Khalifa, Dubai Mall, and Dubai Opera. You'll find a mix of upscale

hotels and serviced apartments within walking distance of these attractions, offering convenience and easy access to shopping, dining, and entertainment.

4. Old Dubai: If you're interested in exploring the historic side of the city, consider staying in Old Dubai. The neighborhoods of Deira and Bur Dubai are rich in culture and heritage. You can find traditional Arabian guesthouses, known as "riads," that provide a glimpse into the city's past.

5. Budget-Friendly Options: Dubai also has a range of budget-friendly accommodations, including affordable hotels and guesthouses. Areas like Al Barsha and Dubai Marina offer more affordable options while still providing easy access to attractions and public transport.

Saving Money Tips

Here are some tips to help you save money during your stay in Dubai:

° Timing is Key: Consider visiting Dubai during the off-peak season, typically from May to September, when hotel rates and airfare prices are lower. Additionally, look for discounted rates during weekdays rather than weekends.

° Public Transportation: Utilize the efficient and affordable public transportation system in Dubai. The Dubai Metro, buses, and trams offer convenient connections to major attractions and areas of the city at a fraction of the cost of taxis. Consider purchasing a Nol card, which provides discounted fares.

° Free Attractions: Dubai has several free attractions that are worth exploring. Visit the historic district of Al Fahidi, stroll along the Dubai Marina Walk, or enjoy the stunning views of the Dubai Fountain show outside the Dubai Mall. Take advantage of these cost-free experiences to immerse yourself in the city's culture and beauty.

° Dining Options: While Dubai is home to many upscale restaurants, there are plenty of affordable dining options as well. Look for local eateries, food courts, and street food stalls where you can sample delicious Arabic cuisine without breaking the bank.

You can also save money by opting for lunchtime deals and set menus at restaurants.

° Shopping Strategies: Dubai is a shopper's paradise, but it's important to be savvy with your purchases. Explore the traditional souks like the Gold Souk and Spice Souk, where you can bargain for unique items and souvenirs. Look out for sales and discounts at malls, and consider visiting outlet stores for discounted designer brands.

° Water and Snacks: Stay hydrated by drinking tap water, which is safe to consume in Dubai. Carry a reusable water bottle and refill it throughout the day. Pack some snacks for when you're out and about to avoid expensive impulse purchases.

FAQ

Q: What is the best time to visit Dubai?
A: The best time to visit Dubai is during the winter months from November to April when the weather is pleasant and ideal for outdoor activities. However, it's important to note that this is also the peak tourist season, so expect larger crowds and higher prices.

Q: What is the currency used in Dubai?

A: The currency used in Dubai is the UAE Dirham (AED). It is recommended to carry some local currency for small purchases and to be prepared for cash-only transactions in certain establishments. ATMs are widely available throughout the city for convenient currency exchange.

Q: Is it safe to travel to Dubai?

A: Dubai is considered a safe city for travelers. It has a low crime rate, and the local authorities prioritize the safety and security of residents and tourists. However, as with any destination, it's always important to exercise common sense and take necessary precautions to ensure your personal safety and belongings.

Q: What is the dress code in Dubai?

A: Dubai follows a modest dress code, especially in public areas and religious sites. It is advisable to dress conservatively and avoid wearing revealing or offensive clothing. When visiting mosques or religious places, both men and women are expected to cover their shoulders, arms, and legs.

Q: Can I consume alcohol in Dubai?

A: Alcohol consumption is allowed in licensed venues such as bars, clubs, and hotels. However, it is important to note that public drunkenness and drinking in public places are strictly prohibited. Non-Muslim residents and tourists can purchase alcohol from licensed stores after obtaining a personal liquor license.

Q: Is it necessary to tip in Dubai?

A: Tipping in Dubai is not mandatory but is appreciated for good service. It is customary to leave a tip of around 10-15% of the total bill at restaurants. Some hotels and restaurants may include a service charge, so it's advisable to check the bill before tipping.

Q: Is it necessary to have travel insurance for Dubai?

A: While travel insurance is not a legal requirement for entering Dubai, it is highly recommended. Travel insurance provides coverage for medical emergencies, trip cancellations, lost luggage, and other unforeseen circumstances that may occur during your trip.

Conclusion

Dubai is a destination that offers a unique blend of luxury, culture, adventure, and architectural wonders. It is a city that captivates visitors with its awe-inspiring skyline, opulent hotels, vibrant souks, and rich cultural heritage. Whether you're seeking an indulgent shopping spree, thrilling outdoor activities, or a journey into history and tradition, Dubai has something to offer every traveler.

This travel guide, "DUBAI TRAVEL GUIDE 2023," serves as your essential companion to navigate the city and immerse yourself in the best that Dubai has to offer. From insider tips and local secrets to recommendations on accommodations, dining, and attractions, this guide provides you with the knowledge and resources to make the most of your Dubai experience.

Discover the iconic landmarks like the Burj Khalifa and Burj Al Arab, explore the traditional souks and markets, and indulge in the exquisite dining scene that Dubai has to offer. Unveil the culture and traditions of the Emirati people, visit historical sites such as the Dubai Museum and Jumeirah Mosque, and venture beyond Dubai to explore nearby destinations like Abu Dhabi, Sharjah, and Al Ain.

Whether you're a first-time visitor or a seasoned traveler, Dubai will leave you in awe of its grandeur, hospitality, and limitless possibilities. Soak in the sunshine, marvel at architectural marvels, savor the flavors of Emirati cuisine, and create memories that will last a lifetime.

With this comprehensive guide in hand, you can confidently navigate Dubai's vibrant streets, discover hidden gems, and make the most of your journey. So, pack your bags, embark on a captivating adventure, and let Dubai's charm and allure take you on a remarkable journey of luxury, culture, and adventure.

Final Thoughts and Recommendations

To make the most of your visit to Dubai, it is recommended to plan your trip in advance and take advantage of the insider tips and local secrets provided in this guide. From choosing the best time to visit to exploring the city's diverse attractions and experiencing its thrilling adventures, this guide equips you with the knowledge and insights you need to create unforgettable memories.

While Dubai is known for its luxury, it is important to respect the local customs and traditions. Dress modestly when visiting religious sites and public areas, and be mindful of local customs and etiquette. Additionally, ensure you have the necessary travel documentation and understand the entry requirements to avoid any complications during your trip.

Dubai's efficient public transportation system makes getting around the city convenient, but it is also worth considering car rentals or private transportation options for more flexibility. Don't forget to stay connected with internet and communication services, as well as ensuring you have appropriate travel insurance for peace of mind.

Lastly, immerse yourself in the vibrant culture and explore the hidden gems that Dubai has to offer. Engage with locals, try traditional Emirati dishes, and discover the city's thriving art and design scene. Embrace the adventure and make the most of your time in this incredible city.

Making the Most of Your Dubai Experience

To make the most of your Dubai experience, it's important to embrace the city's unique blend of luxury, culture, and adventure. Here are some tips to help you maximize your time in this captivating destination.

First and foremost, plan your itinerary wisely. Dubai offers a wide array of attractions and activities, so research and prioritize the ones that align with your interests. Whether it's exploring iconic landmarks, indulging in shopping sprees, or immersing yourself in cultural experiences, having a well-planned itinerary ensures you don't miss out on the highlights.

Take advantage of insider tips and local secrets. This guide provides valuable insights to help you uncover hidden gems and off-the-beaten-path experiences. From lesser-known attractions to authentic dining spots, these recommendations offer a deeper and more authentic understanding of Dubai.

Immerse yourself in the local culture. Dubai is a melting pot of different nationalities and traditions. Engage with locals, visit traditional markets, and attend cultural events to gain a deeper appreciation for the city's heritage.

Indulge in the culinary delights of Dubai. The city boasts a diverse and vibrant food scene, offering everything from traditional Emirati dishes to international cuisines. Explore local eateries, try street food, and savor the flavors that Dubai has to offer.

Stay open-minded and embrace new experiences. Dubai is a city that continuously evolves, offering new attractions and experiences. Be willing to step out of your comfort zone and try something different, whether it's skydiving over Palm Jumeirah or enjoying a desert safari.

Printed in Great Britain
by Amazon